THE DELL WAR SERIES

The Dell War Series takes you onto the battlefield, into the jungles, and beneath the oceans with unforgettable stories that offer a new look at the terrors and triumphs of America's war experience. Many of these books are eyewitness accounts of the duty-bound fighting man. From the intrepid foot soldiers, sailors, pilots, and commanders to the elite warriors of the Special Forces, here are stories of men who fight because their lives depend on it.

☆☆☆☆☆☆☆

ASSAULT ON CAMP A-242

Tuan, the lone-surviving interpreter, crawled through the small hole in the ground where his bunker had been. He looked all around at the carnage and heard the moans and screams of dying people everywhere. He spotted the two Vietnamese traitors and felt a deep hatred welling up in his chest. An NVA soldier ran beside him in the darkness, and Tuan stuck out his arm and tripped the sapper. He was on him in a millisecond, his Montagnard knife flashing in the moonlight. It passed through the soldier's Adam's apple. Tuan took the man's AK, checked the chamber, and flipped it on automatic.

He stood up and walked slowly forward, barefooted and bare-chested, not caring whether he was going to live or die. . . .

QUANTITY SALES

Most Dell books are available at special quantity discounts when purchased in bulk by corporations, organizations, or groups. Special imprints, messages, and excerpts can be produced to meet your needs. For more information, write to: Dell Publishing, 666 Fifth Avenue, New York, NY 10103. Attention: Director, Diversified Sales.

Please specify how you intend to use the books (e.g., promotion, resale, etc.).

INDIVIDUAL SALES

Are there any Dell books you want but cannot find in your local stores? If so, you can order them directly from us. You can get any Dell book currently in print. For a complete up-to-date listing of our books and information on how to order, write to: Dell Readers Service, Box DR, 666 Fifth Avenue, New York, NY 10103.

The B-52 OVERTURE

The North Vietnamese Assault on Special Forces Camp A-242, Dak Pek

DON BENDELL

A DELL BOOK

Published by
Dell Publishing
a division of
Bantam Doubleday Dell Publishing Group, Inc.
666 Fifth Avenue
New York, New York 10103

ISBN: 0-440-21138-7

Printed in the United States of America

Published simultaneously in Canada

July 1992

10 9 8 7 6 5 4 3 2 1

OPM

ACKNOWLEDGMENTS

What can I say about my wife, best friend, business partner, and most honest critic, Shirley, except "Thank you" and "I love you." Thanks, too, to my wonderful editor at Dell, E. J. McCarthy, my agent, Mike Hamilburg, and my manager, Dan Mark.

But the people I want to thank the most in this book are retired Master Sergeant Don "Commo Willy" Williams, and retired or former sergeants and sergeants major Charlie Telfair, Jim Hale, Bobby Stewart, Chuck Challela, Mike Holland, Tom Weeks, Joe Howard, Larry Crotsley, and all the other professional Special Forces NCOs who kept a young, immature, but very gung ho Green Beret lieutenant from coming home in a body bag. This book is for all those NCOs who took young, and old, officers under their wings and made a lot of them look good and kept us alive. Thanks.

To the Montagnards:
You were America's most loyal and staunchest allies.
Today you are being decimated and annihilated and
nobody seems to notice, but I will never forget you,
nor will any SF who lived with you.

*Every ghost I knew marched through me that night,
from the Yang, the spirits of the mountains, to the
company of my dead friends.
It wasn't frightening—sort of cozy, in a grim way.
It was always Halloween in Vietnam.*

JIM MORRIS
"The Devil's Secret Name"

SONS OF THE MOUNTAINS

The Annam came and stole your lands.
They shackled slave chains to your hands.
Oh, how you've died, my warrior friends.
In needless hate-filled bloody ends.

Your sisters raped and daughters, too.
I cry, the things they've done to you.
Stieng, Biat, the Ra, Kaho,
The Gar, Rolom, Chrau Jro, Pacoh,

Todra, Monom, Bahnar, Jarai,
Katua, Sedang, Hre, Hrov, Roglai,
Chru, and the Rengao, Kayong,
Sedang, Duan, Cua, Phuong,

The Brou, Mnong, and the Rade,
Katu, Takua, Halong, and Jeh
So many tribes of Dega proud,
So many live inside a cloud,

A cloud of fear and loss of dreams,
A fog that's filled with dying screams.
Oh, Sons of Mountains, Sisters, too,
The world will hear this song of you,

Yes, some of you are in the ground
But God will strike your enemies down,
For you have lived upon His land
And touched it with a caring hand.

You fought for freedom, never greed,
And fought for peace and family need.
You've played and prayed and worked the sod.
Montagnards, you've lived for God.

—DON BENDELL

1

Flying Within the Cage

I PULLED A Lucky Strike out of the plastic protective
case in the pocket of my fatigue pants, turned the cigarette so the printing on it would be facing out, and
tapped the short cig on the side of my Zippo lighter. I
offered one to the second louey seated next to me and
gave him a light. I lighted my own, then snapped the lid
shut almost in the face of another lieutenant leaning
across the floor of the deuce-and-a-half truck, a Marlboro
sticking out of his mouth.

"What the fuck you doing, Bendell? Can't you give
me a fucking light, too?" the young officer snapped.

I grinned and reopened the lighter by squeezing
tightly on the lid and then snapping my fingers along the
side. I again snapped the fingers on my right hand, my
middle finger spinning the little steel wheel, and a spray
of sparks shot out from the flint. The wick burst into a
flame that illuminated the nervous faces of all the other
lieutenants in the back of the big Army truck. Like me,
each wore a green beret with a gold bar in the middle of
the unit flash. Most wore the same red flash as I, for the
Seventh Special Forces Group, but a few wore the mul-
ticolored flash of the Third Group and a few more wore
the black-and-red flash that designated the Third Group.
They all knew that each would soon be wearing the white-
bordered black flash with the yellow diagonal stripe in it
with three thin red stripes running through that, taken
from the flag of the Republic of South Vietnam.

Like me most of these young men had an MOS of
31542, which meant Special Forces/Airborne-qualified Infantry Officer. Most would leave their next assignment in

a body bag, although some would still be there in a dank underground prison, after more than twenty years, wondering how their country could forget about them. Still more would simply become part of the decaying countryside of tropical Vietnam, replenishing the soil, to grow more countryside that could be destroyed as easily by the greed and avarice of men.

By way of explanation, I grinned at the offended lieutenant and said, "Superstition man—started in World War Two. Never light more than two cigarettes on a match. Gives a sniper time to zero in on your running lights."

Still angry, or more likely nervous as hell, the lieutenant snapped, "Ain't no snipers in the back of this fucking vehicle, man."

I stared into the other officer's eyes and said, "Lighten up."

"Fuck you!" the man replied, his face obviously reddening visibly, even in the darkness of the truck.

"Fuck you, too, and the horse you rode in on," I answered, grinning.

The young man started to jump across the truck but was restrained by two friends.

He snapped, "I ought to kick your tall, skinny ass, Bendell."

"You ought to bring your lunch and at least five friends, pal, 'cause it will be an all-day affair," I replied. "I think you're just lashing out at me anyway, because you're a pussy and afraid you're going to get your balls chopped off by Charlie. Why don't you cool off and act like a leader?"

We two lieutenants felt the butterflies and quivers inside our systems that came before combat. We were like two young bulls in a harem of elk, not quite ready yet to take on the old monarch, but full of piss and vinegar, and ready to fight something, maybe anything. We strutted and hid our apprehension behind masks of bravado.

Then both of us, truly wanting to be respected leaders as well as warriors, seemed to realize we were of the same herd and needed to fight predators and not each other.

I looked down the length of the truck and saw the faces of two guys who had spent the past year with me, Tom Eggers and Phil Bauso.

Eggers was short and bowlegged, and he still carried his perpetual tan from Florida. He was in a different company in the Seventh Group, but had graduated from Infantry OCS at Fort Benning, Georgia, in my unit: 56th Company, class of June 1967. I got hospitalized during tower week in jump school with double pneumonia and pleurisy, and Eggers and Phil Bauso visited me at Martin Army Hospital, teasing me unmercifully about getting recycled and having to take jump school all over again. The following day, Eggers reached into a shed to pick up a parachute harness and got bitten on the back of his hand by a rattlesnake. He ended up in Martin Army Hospital on the same floor I was on. He, too, got recycled.

Bauso was an ideal candidate for Special Forces, the unit of mavericks and unusual characters. He was rumored to have been an attorney in New York and could have joined the Army with a direct commission as a captain in the Judge Advocate General's corps, but instead he joined as a private, went to Infantry OCS, and was commissioned an infantry second lieutenant.

"If any of us get captured," Eggers said, "don't give in to them if they try to make you do push-ups or anything, or they'll keep making you do other things!"

All the officers in the packed truck looked, plain-faced, at him while he spoke.

One said, "How do you know, Eggers?"

"My buddy was a POW," he replied. "Once he started following their orders, they kept making more and more demands on him. They also hooked wires up to his balls, then asked him questions. Ole Victor Charlie turned the crank on a field phone to encourage him to answer properly, too."

The Marlboro smoker traded seats with the guy next to me and leaned over, smiling, "Sorry, man, I didn't mean to get pissed like that."

I grinned and said, "Forget it. We have the most dangerous MOS in 'Nam: We both know almost every man in the back of this truck is going to get zapped."

The two of us somberly surveyed the truckload of Special Forces junior officers. We realized the truth of my words. Within a year, the survivors of that group would hardly fill the seats in a jeep. Both of us tried to think of something clever to say to cover our fear. Instead, we replaced our macho veneers, a necessary survival technique in our occupation.

Marlboro man said, "Fuck them, man, I'm coming back."

I laughed, "Well, if you don't, don't worry, I'll be porking your old lady."

The other officer chuckled and replied, "Sure, go ahead, if you don't mind all that used pussy."

I grinned again and said, "I'm sure it won't be bad once I get past the used part."

The guy good-heartedly punched me on the bicep. I looked past him and settled on Lieutenant Leopold. Leopold wasn't laughing and chattering like his comrades that night. Apparently deep in thought, a faraway look in his eyes, he leaned forward on the barrel of his M-16, oblivious of the talking of his buddies around him. Then something else strange struck me: just beyond Leopold was Heinz Roesch, acting exactly the same way. Seeing the two men sitting there silently staring off into space gave me a shiver down my spine.

Numerous intelligence reports indicated there were enemy patrols all over that area. The truck was filled with Special Forces officers. What better target could the Vietcong pick for destruction or capture? Besides that, another truckload of lieutenants had already been captured and hauled away to a POW camp by the black-pajama-clad soldiers with the little pointed straw hats.

Normally the young SF officers would have all been jabbering continuously, trying to pretend we were not humans. In fact, all around Leopold and Roesch, lieutenants were yakking incessantly, bragging about eating bar glasses the night before, or rapelling down the side of their apartment building at a drunken party in Fayetteville. These young men certainly did party hard. In our time off, many of us got drunk and went skydiving or looked for big buildings to rappel off of.

Just a week before, most of us were drinking in the officers' club one night, laughing our heads off when we watched the national news with Chet Huntley and David Brinkley.

The last news item of the night was read by Chet Huntley, who said; "Three Green Beret lieutenants were arrested at a very wild party in Fayetteville, North Carolina, this past weekend."

One of the young men raised his glass and shouted, "Hey, we made the national news, everybody!"

All of us raised our glasses, cheered, and gulped down our drinks.

Two of the group threw the party and moved all the furniture from their furnished apartment into other apartments, leaving only mattresses in the three bedrooms. A band played loudly in the living room and several large metal trash cans were filled with ice and bottles of booze in the kitchen. They were quickly emptied and refilled, over and over again. The police were summoned three different times to the plush Tarrytown Apartment complex, before the arrests were finally made.

A very drunken yours truly was almost arrested when a policeman caught me making out with my date, a high school Spanish teacher, on the hood of a police cruiser, but I lucked out.

Several of the drunken partygoers were Green Beret colonels and majors and the rest were company grade officers. The field grades saved the bacon of the junior officers and persuaded General Flanagan at JFK Center to make the problem go away as quickly as possible.

These young lieutenants were all going to Vietnam to serve as XOs on Special Forces A-teams, mike forces, and with MAC-V SOG.

SOG was the top secret unit comprised primarily of Special Forces men, but with its members wearing "sterile" uniforms and using "sterile" equipment as they ran very deep penetrations into North Vietnam, Laos, and Cambodia. They primarily went on recon patrols with six-man RTs (recon teams) comprised of two Americans and four mercenaries. Sometimes they went on "snatch missions" to purposely locate and capture a prisoner for updating intelligence, or they also went on direct action missions, such as sabotage. Other guys served on "hatchet teams," primarily assigned to go into a really hot fight to extract the little RTs out of a big mess.

All of us were being assigned to the most dangerous jobs in Vietnam. The fact that we were with the best-trained, sharpest NCOs in any military force in the world was the primary reason that any of us did live.

Most of us had graduated from OCS and were not only confronting death but also felt the pressure of trying to be placed in command positions with such good NCOs. We wanted to measure up to the hero image of Special Forces. John Wayne was in the process of making the much-publicized movie *The Green Berets,* based on Robin Moore's best seller. Special Forces Sergeant Barry Sadler had recorded the number one hit song "Ballad of the Green Berets." Some of these young officers had been in high school just a year or two before, and now we were stopped on the street and asked for our autographs. World War II vets bought us drinks. Women offered us their bodies.

We could not show the fear that we all felt: not the fear of death—it was the fear of failure, the fear of not living up to the image. The NCOs didn't help either. Almost all of them lived up to the image. And so, the image, the public and self-preception of this superhero fighting force did, in fact, create many heros. One and all tried beyond normal endeavor to measure up to an ideal that was almost too high, buoyed by the successes of those who already "walked point" before them.

The image certainly created heroes, but it created tremendous pressures on us as well. How did we handle it? We partied hard. We drank hard. We worked hard. We studied hard. And when some did die: most of us died hard.

The truck passed quickly through a grove of vine-covered hardwoods, and a shadowy figure sat on an overhanging branch as we passed beneath. In the darkness of the night something shone in his hand as he brought it up to his face. It was the microphone of a radio. He sent a quick message to his pajama-clad comrades down the road.

A good-looking, blue-eyed, blond, Dan Cahoon, shouted above the rumbling of the truck, "Hey, you guys hear about Frank Van Hoy?"

Just a couple of months before, Frank and his wife and another couple had seen North Carolina's mysterious "Maco light," and he had been amazed by it. Frank, with his ever-present smile, spoke with wonder about seeing this myserious light travel down a section of old railroad tracks, in southeast North Carolina, and illuminate the inside of his car, while the foursome watched from a nearby hillside. It then took off and disappeared. If Frank hadn't been SF himself, maybe the others wouldn't have paid much attention.

"What about him?" someone else asked, but nobody really wanted to know.

Frank was popular among the young officers, and if

something happened to him, it would remind one and all of their own mortality and vulnerability.

Dan answered, "I heard he got assigned to an A-team in I Corps [pronounced "eye"] and his camp got hit. He was on-site less than twenty-four hours and a fuckin' mortar round landed in a foxhole with him."

"Fuck!" I yelled. "Frank got killed?"

"No!" Cahoon responded, "he got wounded and got medevacked back to 'the World,' but I heard he's going to be okay."

Everyone seemed to suddenly cheer up. It was almost recognizable in the whole group simultaneously.

The man continued, "That's nothing: Frank's already talking about going to flight school and going back over as a chopper pilot!"

The mood got elevated again and the discussion went to chopper pilots. We discussed the differences between Hueys and Cobras, slick pilots and gunship pilots.

Two of the officers got into a disagreement over emergency procedures in helicopters.

The shorter one said, "Bullshit! If the engine goes out on a chopper, and it's over a hundred feet up, it can autorotate."

The other said, "How, if the engine's not running?"

The first replied, "They do it to rotary pilots in flight school."

"Do what?" someone else asked.

Shorty responded, "The instructor makes them hover up about a grand and then shuts the chopper down. The student has to autorotate it down safely. The air pressure makes the rotors spin. He hits on the back of his skids and pushes forward; just as he touches down, the ship skids forward."

Eggers said, "What if the student flunks the test?"

All the men laughed.

Dan Cahoon laughed and said, "You know what's

the last thing that goes through the student's mind if he flunks?"

"What?"

"His asshole!"

Everyone roared.

Wham! Explosions! Confusion! The truck skidded to a stop in a cloud of dust, and the whole group moaned as our collective bodies were mashed together toward the front of the truck by centrifugal force. Each man tried to swallow but couldn't. As quickly as the brakes were applied, we all seemed to run out of saliva too. There was a deafening chatter of bullets outside in the darkness, mixed with assorted voices, speaking Vietnamese. Then complete silence.

The officers looked at one another, our eyes searching faces for some magical answer to get us the hell out of this situation. We hid our emotions behind our macho masks, but every one of us felt a tremendous pounding in our ears: our heartbeats. The silence was broken by the sounds of first one and then all the officers cocking their M-16 rifles. We sat on the edge of the benches, ready to launch ourselves into a desperation fight for survival, but nobody moved. We were all unsure of whether we should attack or counterpunch. More overwhelming, deafening silence. One man farted. A nervous chuckle.

Suddenly we jumped as a loud voice outside boomed, "Fucking American Green Berets! *Lai de mau! Lai de mau!* Truck surrounded! Have *beaucoup* VC! Come out! Hands up! Come out, you shoot! All die! Number ten!"

The two men closest to the rear of the Army truck pulled back the flap and peeked out. They both shook their heads, handed their rifles out, stood, and placed their hands on top of their heads, fingers interlocked. As the two men carefully sat on the edge of the truck's tailgate and swung their legs out, several pairs of hands appeared, grabbing them by the arms and pulling them into the darkness. The silence in the truck was now no longer a tense silence of apprehension: it was a defeated, heart-wrenching silence of resignation. Seeing the actions of the first two, the others followed suit, already knowing that either fight or flight was obviously hopeless.

Before climbing out, I peeked under the edge of the canvas and saw black-pajamaed enemy soldiers everywhere. I dropped my rifle, quickly pulled my Ka-bar knife from its sheath, and slipped it up my right sleeve, where I held it in place with my fingers. With my left hand, I pulled my matches, little compass, and pocketknife out of my pockets and dropped them down the front of my fatigue uniform. I sat on the edge of the tailgate and swung my legs out into the night air.

Rough hands grabbed me and yanked me into the darkness. I hit the ground with a thud and was slammed face first into the soft dirt. My wrists were cuffed tightly behind my back and an Army bandage was tied around my eyes. A piece of nylon parachute suspension line was tied to the belt loop of my right hip. This line was also tied to the belt loops of the men in front of and behind me. The line of blindfolded prisoners was led through the thick forest.

Miraculously, my blindfold was crooked, and I could see with my right eye by tilting my head upward. Letting the knife slip down into my hand, I sawed on the parachute suspension cord. It barely cut through the tough cord. *Son of a bitch,* I thought. I had put off sharpening the blade after coming back from a recent FTX (field training exercise). Still sawing, I kept tilting my head up to check out the black-garbed guards leading the group through the woods. They hadn't spotted my actions, so I desperately sawed on the line.

The line of prisoners stumbled down into a shallow ravine, traversed its length for a short distance, then scrambled and fell up the opposite bank, a short distance from a group of tents, two machine-gun towers with searchlights, more guards, and a square-shaped POW compound with a small shack within. The camp was enclosed by two twelve-foot-high barbed-wire fences with an eight-foot corridor in between, filled to the top by rows of triple-strand concertina wire. Additionally, two sections within the compound, in the front corners, were enclosed by small movable barbed-wire fences, and both sectors contained two large unpitched canvas tents.

"Shit," I whispered to myself, sawing even more frantically on the line.

Knowing we would be at the POW camp in seconds, I planted my feet and gave a final desperate lunge backward. The rope didn't break and several blindfolded men in front of me fell on their backs along with me as the suspension line held.

"Oh, fuck me," I muttered audibly, knowing that I was in serious trouble.

The blood drained out of my head, and I felt a little faint, as I heard a deep belly laugh directly behind me and a pair of oversized hands, more like vises, grabbed me by the shoulders and effortlessly jerked me to my feet. It was the head guard. A behemoth, he had apparently been behind me the whole time, enjoying the show of my trying to saw through my bonds.

Grabbing the knife from me, he curled the line into a little loop, stuck the dull blade inside it, and gave it a jerk. The blade passed cleanly through the cord, and the big brute laughed heartily.

"Big ugly motherfucker aren't you?" I said, "I thought you were supposed to be short little yellow fuckers."

The guard spoke in broken English, "I speak English, too, Chicago gangster."

My eyes opened wide, and I said, "Oh, shit."

Grabbing me by the arm, King Kong escorted me, on my tiptoes, to a place by the tents where the prisoners were already being given instructions to process in. I started shivering uncontrollably and finally noticed how cold it was.

I muttered, "I thought this area was supposed to be a hot and humid weather area, too. It's colder than a penguin's pecker."

Like the others, I wore only fatigues, a pack, and an ammo harness. The harnesses, packs, and M-16s had already been confiscated, and now the group was told to strip. The young men stood, buck naked, in the middle of the thick wet greenery on the coldest night of the year, wondering what other horrors lay ahead for us. It was not the hot flat rice paddies of the Mekong Delta either.

Our socks, underwear, T-shirts, belts, bootlaces, dog tags, and valuables were confiscated and placed in manila envelopes labeled with the name, rank, and serial number of each prisoner. We were told to turn our fatigues inside out and put them on. Next, the group of frightened prisoners were told to get in line at a large folding table, three abreast, where we were handed pens and told to sign the manila envelopes containing our valuables.

I gulped, knowing I was going to refuse to sign for my valuables. In code-of-conduct classes it had been drummed into our heads to never sign any kind of document if we became prisoners of war. I was scared, but when my turn came, I stepped up to the table, took the pen in my hand, and lunged across the table at the seated guard. King Kong, however, somehow sensed my plan and waited for me. He slammed a beefy forearm across my windpipe and viciously lifted me off the ground. My right arm was twisted behind my back in a tendon-stretching hammerlock.

The head guard spoke in a deep voice. "You sign envelope now."

"Fuck you!" I gasped in anger, "You Communist cocksucker!"

I couldn't breathe as the moose leg of an arm squeezed across my throat. My body was swung around and slammed against a very large, very hard tree. A pair of handcuffs appeared in the big guard's hands and were snapped around my thin wrists, after my arms were stretched around the tree. I watched as the others came up and signed their individual envelopes.

I shouted, "Hey, you guys, don't sign anything! They'll use our signatures!"

King Kong appeared again out of nowhere with an Army bandage in his hand and shoved it into my mouth, tying the cloth ends around my head. I tried in vain to use my teeth and tongue to push the cotton gauze pad out, but my efforts were in vain. Every few minutes the head guard walked by me with the deep bass chuckle rumbling out of his barrel chest.

I was uncuffed after everyone finished processing. Our ammo harnesses, backpacks, and rifles were tagged and locked in the wooden shed. We were divided into two groups and placed in the two sections of the camp that contained the unpitched tents. Instead of pitching the tents, even though we were freezing, we climbed under the canvas and huddled together, arms around one another, hoping our collective body warmth would provide some comfort against the cold.

Then the music started. A number of large loud-speakers were right outside the fence of each sector aimed in at the camp at ground level. Those speakers blared Vietnamese music full blast. That was followed by loud psychedelic noises, sound effects, and even more Vietnamese music. The decibel level must have been somewhere between that of the inside of an engine in a B-52 taking off and a high-yield nuclear bomb. There would be no rest for the wicked that night, or the angelic, for that matter.

Each man huddled under the tent, his arms wrapped around the man in front of him, his body pressed tightly against the other's back, another man's arms wrapped around him. I couldn't help chuckling.

A voice asked. "Who's that?"

"It's Bendell. I was just wondering what would happen if one of us gets a hard-on."

Nervous laughter.

Another lieutenant said, "He's gonna be one dead faggot."

Everyone laughed, relieving the tension.

The music stopped.

A voice came over the loudspeakers: King Kong again. "Assemble for roll call!"

The prisoners scrambled out of our giant canvas wombs and faced the chilly midnight cold. The two groups lined up in ranks and stood at attention. The head guard sat at a table just outside the main gate. The searchlights from the guard towers were blinding.

The deep voice rumbled again as King Kong called out the names of four prisoners, "You all try escape! Number ten! Walk to gate!"

One of the lieutenants fell for the mind-blowing psychological ploy and protested, holding his hands out in a pleading gesture. "No! Please, I didn't try to escape! I swear!"

Another lieutenant whispered loudly, "Shut the fuck up, pussy! You're SF! Act like it!"

The young officer realized who he was and where he was and suddenly straightened up, puffing his chest out. He walked to the gate and stood at rigid attention. The four young men were grabbed by guards coming in the gate and three were escorted out the entrance, while the one who pleaded was taken to a gray steel wall locker lying on its side in the middle of the compound. Two guards placed him, kicking and screaming, inside, closed the door, and rolled it over on the door. While he screamed, and we watched in horror, they started beating on the wall locker with two wooden clubs.

The men were dismissed and scrambled back under the tarps, but the loudspeakers were not turned on for a while. Instead, the prisoners were treated to the sounds of the guards beating the wall locker and the man screaming inside. Finally, after half an hour, the banging stopped, and soon afterward I heard the sounds of the man climbing under the tarp and the sounds of subdued sobs. The music started again, but only for fifteen minutes. Another compound formation was called and the men climbed out of the warmth of their hideaways and stood at attention again. More names were called out, including mine. Two of the men called were accused of not having been there for the previous formation.

The giant head guard personally came into the compound, cuffed me, and escorted me out the gate. The man's grip was like the jaws of a great white shark, and the low laugh rumbled every few seconds. He was even larger than Dick "Cherokee" Wright, one of the most respected and the largest of the young lieutenants. I was taken to a tent and led inside.

A smiling Caucasian man sat behind a table on a folding chair. He wore a nondescript brown uniform with a white arm band with a red cross on it. I was cuffed to a folding chair across from the man and pushed onto the seat. The man shooed Goliath out and stuck his hand across the table at me, and we shook hands.

"Carter, International Red Cross," the man said, "Cigarette?"

I accepted the Pall Mall cigarette and light the man offered me. I dragged deeply and watched with curiosity as Carter bent over, picked up a cardboard box, and placed it on the table in front of me. He carefully pulled out the contents and displayed them on the table. There was a variety of toiletries, some playing cards, stationery, and a pen.

The man spoke too cheerfully, "Here's a Care package for you from the Red Cross, and we want to notify your family right away that you've been captured."

"Great," I said tentatively.

The man had a phony smile and wouldn't look me in the eye.

Carter set a form and a pen down in front of me and continued, "We just need you to sign for your package right here."

"Fuck you," I said, "I sign nothing. Red Cross, my ass, you phony fucking traitor."

The squirrel kept grinning and said, "Now see here. I'm not the enemy. I want to help you."

"You mean that?"

"Yes, I do."

"Fine," I replied. "You don't have to even remove these cuffs. Just turn your back for a ten count, and the chair and I will disappear."

The man kept grinning and yelled, "Guard!"

Mighty Joe Young again. He unlocked the cuff, quickly removed me from the tent, and took me to the next tent, which was labeled CAMP COMMANDER.

Viet King Cong said, "Request permission to enter camp commander's tent."

I sneered, "Eat shit and die, you fucking gook."

He slapped me on the back of the head and said, "Request permission to enter camp commander's tent!"

I had learned from NCOs that the Vietnamese respected and feared extreme toughness. I also figured I was in a "no win" situation anyway, so I smiled up at him and spit right in the guard's face. The big man's face got red, and he balled his hand into a fist, but just as quickly he stopped himself and wiped the spittle off his face. He half carried, half dragged me to a nearby tree, cuffed me to it, and simply walked away.

I wished I were thinner, as I spit on my hand and tried to slip one of the cuffs over it, only to get it stuck just above the knuckles. It felt as if my hand were wedged in an escalator. I pulled, fidgeted, winced in pain, and finally slipped the cuff back over my wrist.

Next I used my cuffed hands to pull, as I shinnied up

the sapling and clung to it like some kind of smooth-skinned giant human sloth. I was clinging there, twenty feet up, when the head guard returned, looked up, and started laughing again.

The monster spoke. "What you do, make cuffs pass through branches? Yankee, you *dinky dau.*"

I knew more torture and uncertainty waited for me twenty feet below, but I clung to my perch. Finally, though, my strength gave out and I slid down to the ground—and yet another unknown but frightening fate. King Kong again unlocked a cuff and dragged me back inside the compound, where we were greeted by two other guards.

The head one spoke, "He *beaucoups* cold. Put him in building. Make him warm."

The laugh again.

I was knocked down, seized, and shoved inside the wall locker. It was rolled over on the door. They started beating on it with clubs. At first I was too angry to be frightened.

Inside the locker, I squeezed my arms against my sides, slid them up to my head, and plugged my ears with my fingers. I felt my heart pounding and my chest heaved in and out.

I remembered an operation, some months earlier, where I was in a culvert pipe tunnel, dressed in black pajamas myself. The Third Infantry Regiment, Washington, DC's "Old Guard," were taking their ATT (annual training test) to check their combat effectiveness. My team were the Vietcong and had, up to that point, been humiliating one particular company from the Third. This was a set operation, however, as the team members were required to hide in a network of tunnels that were ten feet under a mock Vietnamese village built by SF at Camp A. P. Hill, Virginia.

I crawled down one narrow culvert pipe, planning to wait under the trapdoor that came out under the main village cooking fire. At a tunnel intersection almost directly below the escape hatch, someone had thrown a gas grenade. I crawled into the area and my face, tongue, lungs, and hands started burning as if acid had been thrown on me. Somehow, fighting panic and blinded, I hooked my toes in the culvert pipe ripples and crawled backward. Miraculously, I made it and was eventually rescued by other team members.

A CBN, or chemical-biological-nuclear investigation team, was immediately brought down from the Pentagon. Since my clothes were already contaminated, they had me crawl back into the tunnel carrying an air-testing device and wearing rubber gloves, boots, hood, and protective mask. I took an air sample and brought it and the expended grenade out. The meter indicated that the gas was right on the line between CS and mustard gas. They concluded the grenade had been an experimental gas grenade, and nobody could figure out how somebody got his hands on it and threw it into the tunnel.

My face was blistered above both eyes and on one cheek, as was my tongue. Having recently recuperated from double pneumonia and pleurisy, I really had a time with my lungs too.

I thought back to the claustrophobic feelings I had in the narrow pipe, crawling out backward, blinded and in pain, worrying about a cave-in, or a rattlesnake crawling up between my legs.

I made it out of the tunnel, and I lived. I'll make this, dammit, I said to myself.

My breathing and heart rate slowed down, but every few minutes I'd have to check myself again, when the panic would start, once more.

The beating stopped, I felt the locker rolling over, and I shivered. Steeling myself for the opening of the door, I shut my eyes quickly. The two guards peered down at me, wondering if my heart might have stopped during the ordeal. I opened my eyes, yawned, and stretched my arms out into the night air.

"Can't you Communist fuckers let a guy get some sleep around here?" I said as if coming out of dreamland itself.

Grabbing my arms, they yanked me to my feet. Neither spoke; one just pointed to the other group of lieutenants across the compound, and I joined the group who were in assembly again but were now being made to do push-ups. King Kong, over the PA system, ordered me to join them, but I flipped the man the finger and stood there. The other lieutenants were told to fall out, and they gladly scrambled under the tarp again. I stood in the cold. I figured by then it must be a few hours before daylight.

I was not being brave: I had figured out the game. The head guard was Master Sergeant Charlie Telfair of Bravo Company, Seventh Special Forces Group. All the SF NCOs running around in black PJs, like Charlie, were watching us young officers, their supposed leader corps. I knew that these NCOs respected anyone with brass balls, so I would play it out to the hilt, although the cold had gotten to me long before, and I wondered if I might die of hypothermia.

Besides, I could look around while standing in the cold and try to figure out an escape plan. Lieutenant Colonel Robert Furman, the CO of Bravo Company, had promised a three-day class-A pass for anyone who could escape his supposedly escape-proof POW camp. My loyalty, however, was to Lieutenant Colonel Richard Reid, the CO of my unit, Charlie Company, especially since the "old man" had escaped the Nazis and E and E'ed (escaped and evaded) through mile after mile of Germany's Black Forest during the "war to end all wars."

More importantly, I wanted the pass.

More than anything, though, I always wanted to prove that a tall, skinny guy could be an officer as well as a hero, a Green Beret, and not the alcoholic, delinquent loser and class clown I had been at Tallmadge and Coventry high schools in Akron, Ohio.

"Lieutenant Hardass." Telfair's voice came over the loudspeaker system. "Are you ready to cooperate?"

I knew that it was Telfair's job to make me cooperate, and I knew that all these SF NCOs didn't want wimp officers wearing the same beret and patch as they did, so they would be as tough as possible, but I also figured, *they can't kill me.* I flipped the big man the finger.

I had taken a course in underwater hand-to-hand combat and Charlie Telfair had been the chief instructor and NCOIC. Like the POW training, Telfair and his sergeants were tough, very tough. The beret meant a lot to them, and they didn't want their officers to own it cheaply. He also wanted as many officers to come back alive as possible. We lieutenants were taught how to fight against a man in scuba gear or snorkel, armed and unarmed, how to swim and survive with our hands bound behind our backs and feet tied together. How to buddy-breathe and fight two men at once underwater.

The training was rough, and I learned then how tough and professional the big man was. I knew I could give Telfair the finger in this situation, or even spit in his catcher's-mitt-size face and be respected for it, but to do it on the street or in a bar—well, that would be like walking up to Muhammad Ali and offering him a quarter for a shoe shine. I respected Charlie Telfair because he was mean and good, and he gave a shit.

I saw Telfair nod at two guards, and they came through the front gate. I was seized by the arms and dragged to a barbed-wire cage, three feet long by two feet high, with a wooden frame door and a lock on it. It was assembled against an oak tree in the middle of the POW camp. I was placed inside the cage and was forced to tuck my knees up into my chest. Snow fell and my teeth chattered, as I listened to the Vietnamese music that was now being distorted by changing tape speeds.

I told myself, *Fucking snow in southern North Carolina and VC that have to buy their black pajamas from Fayetteville Tent and Awning Company. Keep your humor, man. Think about Myrtle Beach. Keep thinking, period.*

Hearing screams, I tried to turn my head. A thin lieutenant from the first tent had crawled out and screamed hysterically. Several guards ran to the front gate and unlocked it. The man stripped off his fatigues and ran, still screaming, toward the barbed-wire perimeter. Blank-loaded M-60 machine guns from both guard towers chattered with rapid fire, but I plainly saw the young man wasn't trying to escape, not really: he had completely lost it.

The guards ran into the compound while the young man impaled his naked body against the tall barbed-wire fence and climbed, blood streaming down his legs. They reached the screaming officer, grabbed his legs, and he defecated and urinated all over them and himself. Charlie Telfair appeared with an army blanket and ran to the man as he was pulled off the wire. He wrapped it around him, and they removed him gently from the camp.

I felt a tear form in my left eye, and roll down my cheek. It froze there.

"Better here than over there—in command," I said out loud, trying to keep my own thinking clear. *If it's this fucking rough in the middle of Fort Bragg, North Carolina, in training—if we are officers of the top fighting force in the world, and we lose it in training, what must it be like for some poor fucker who's simply a corporal or private from some grunt unit. Damn! They can't expect people to just give name, rank, and serial number. It won't work. Keep talking, Bendell, you handsome fucker. Ha, ha. Keep talking. You're beating them.*

I felt my cheek rest in fresh snow, and then there was a siren in the distance. My eyes snapped open. Why were they closed? I struggled for breath, lungs burning. I fainted, I thought. I remembered the young lieutenant having a mental breakdown as I heard the distant siren. They apparently had an ambulance take him to Womack Army Hospital. Wait, I thought, something was wrong. It all came full force into my brain. I had pneumonia again. The music was so loud, I couldn't hear myself think. The sky, through the trees, was turning dark gray with the coming of "false dawn."

Hunching my back against the end of the cage, careful not to have any of the sharp barbs pushing against my skin, I straightened my body, kicking the bottoms of my jungle boots against the two-by-four frame of the cage door, right at the lock. The door crashed open and I struggled out into the middle of another earsplitting round of withering fire of 7.62 mm blanks from the M-60 machine guns in the guard towers. Raising my hands above my head, I walked to the front gate. I felt faint, and the guards wavered in front of my eyes as they ran toward me. The gate was unlocked.

I struggled with the words, "This is administrative, guys. I got pneumonia bad."

The guards took me by the arms and escorted me to a canvas wall tent and dragged me inside. For the first time in hours, I felt some warmth. The giant master sergeant sat on a steel cot and motioned to the base of it.

"Cuff him to the frame," Charlie said. "The doctor's coming after breakfast anyway. One of the guards has pneumonia, too. Get some army blankets and cover him."

I lay on the ground on top of two blankets and was covered with four more. My right arm, cuffed to the steel cot frame, was suspended about six inches up in the air. I struggled for breath.

Telfair lay down on the cot and then his deep voice filtered quietly through the darkness. "Lieutenant, always keep your knife sharp and your gun clean."

I answered quietly, my words hanging in the still air, "I won't forget, Sergeant."

A few hours later, a jungle boot kicked me awake. The Paul Bunyanesque E-8 looked down with an evil grin. Light came through the door of the tent and the sides were now an ugly light green. The tent was surrounded with the sounds of morning. Charlie Telfair had become himself for only seconds, a few hours earlier, but was once again the hardass demanding head guard. He left the tent, and seconds later two guards came in, removed my handcuffs, and shackled my ankles with parachute suspension line.

I was led outside and seated by a roaring fire. Every time the guards looked away, I tried to untie my shackles. A guard walked up with an aluminum tray with scrambled eggs, toast, bacon, and coffee and handed it to me. I started to eat.

Charlie Telfair got on the PA and called for a roll call and formation again. Pieces of toast were thrown over the wire to the freezing lieutenants, who grabbed the food like two packs of hungry dogs.

Telfair grinned and pointed at me, "Last night, Lieutenant Bendell slept with many warm blankets and eats hot food by a fire. He has told us all your plans. He cooperated."

"Fuck you!" I shouted. I jumped up, threw my tray of food at the NCO, and was promptly shoved back down by the fire.

A guard went back for more food and foolishly left his M-14 rifle leaning against the tent closest to the fire. I lunged for the rifle and was struck down by another sergeant. I was placed back on the steel folding chair at the fire. A minute later I stuck my jungle boots in the flames, hoping to burn through the suspension line, but the fire was too hot.

Colonel Furman arrived at the camp, accompanied by several VIPs, and showed them around. They were impressed. I heard the colonel telling the men that the camp was indeed esacpe-proof.

And I said to myself, *Just let me get my legs untied, Bob, and you'll eat those words."*

Two guards came and summoned me and the sick guard to see the doctor, who had arrived. I struggled to my feet and took several hobbling steps forward toward the distant line of tents. The sick guard was in front of me and we moved slowly forward, the two guards behind me engaged in conversation.

Suddenly, I felt freedom of movement in my legs and looked down. Miraculously, the many minutes of working the knots in the hobbles had paid off. The left side of the line came free. I didn't think of pneumonia. I didn't think of pain. I didn't think of the two guards behind me. I thought of two things: Colonel Furman saying that the camp was "escape-proof," and freedom. Pain be damned, my adrenal glands took charge.

I ran like the wind, glancing back occasionally at the two guards in hot pursuit. Passing the row of tents, I heard shouts of anger behind me. I also heard the prisoners cheering.

The guards chased me through the woods yelling, too, but they were definitely not cheering. I just dodged in and out among trees and tried to stay conscious and free. I was no longer being chased by pretend guards, I was being chased by hard-core NVA soldiers. I didn't have pneumonia: I had a chance for freedom.

Wham! With hundreds of thousands of acres of woods in Fort Bragg, North Carolina, I ran right into a line of old rusty triple-strand concertina barbed wire some unit had left in the woods.

I fell upon the sharp wire and cried out in pain, "Oh, fuck!"

Running up behind me, the closest guard laughed triumphantly and yelled, "Escape from me, you cock-sucker."

. He jumped on my back and laughed sadistically, yanking out a pair of handcuffs. The barbed wire stuck deep in my chest, arms, legs, and hip. My fatigue uniform was torn to shreds, and I felt myself being jerked up off the wire. Blood soaked into my uniform. Barely able to speak, I grinned and said in a half whisper, "Cocksucker, *sir,* you unprofessional son of a bitch!"

The two embarassed NCO-guards dragged me back to the compound, while I struggled to breathe and focus my eyes, but I found no difficulty smiling. An hour later I awakened in Womack Army Hospital, but I had a three-day class-A pass. Another lieutenant escaped an hour after me.

One memory remained burned in my mind from the experience. It was the sight of Lieutenants Roesch and Leopold staring into space amid the nervous young officers chattering in the back of the truck.

Two memories actually: The other was Charlie Telfair's words about keeping my knife sharp and my gun clean.

2

Yards

MUA SAT DOWN in the middle of the fast-running, crystal-clear river and scooped up ice-cold water in her little copper hands, dripping it on her firm breasts. She lifted up the bar of soap she had been given by the American medic and soaped the two large mounds. Her nipples stood out sharply because of the chilly water and early morning breeze.

The area was the most mountainous in Vietnam and the fast-moving water was indeed chilly, even if afternoon temperatures soared to over one hundred degrees with incredibly high humidity. The mountains made the nights very cold, and that also affected the water's temperature.

Cold or not, Mua was glad to get away from her family for a while and often came down the hill to the river for a bath at sunrise. She had seen a magazine an American owned and pretended she was bathing in a bubble bath like one she saw in a picture. Mua liked to daydream about falling in love with an American as Ning, the beautiful woman from the village of Dak Tung, had. She looked up at her village, Dak Jel Luk, perched atop the nearest hill, and fantasized about some handsome American Green Beret taking her away from her toils, fears, and primitive lifestyle, into a world of luxury and excitement. She pictured a handsome American taking her into his bunker, and she reached down under the water and touched her private part, the part she had been saving for some noble and courageous warrior.

Mua was a member of the Jeh tribe, and their village was in the valley where the Dak Pek flowed into the mighty Dak Poko, in which she now bathed and fondled herself. She closed her eyes and breathed heavily through her nose, trying to picture what it would be like the first time with the man of her dreams. Elders told her that what she was doing with her fingers would cause severe pimples, but she knew better, and right now she didn't care. Mua figured it was worth it.

The sounds of three men laughing brought her eyes open and caused a whimper to escape her pouting lips. Three Vietnamese soldiers stood in the bushes along the river's bank and chuckled as they held up her *atok,* the black silk wraparound skirt that Montagnard women wore. Because of comments made by American and Vietnamese soldiers, some Jeh women even started wearing shirts given them by missionaries to cover their breasts, but Mua thought that silly.

She wanted to yell, but one of the soldiers pointed a rifle at her and made a shushing gesture with his finger. He signaled to her to come to him, but she hesitated. Another raised his rifle and pointed it at her.

Mua cried inside, but decided she would not show any fear to the *Yuan.* Her father wouldn't, nor would her brothers. She knew what would happen when she reached the bank and the thick bushes obscuring the possibility of any view from the village. She would no longer be fresh for her man when she met him. She also knew that her father and brothers would be killed trying to get revenge if she told anyone, so she would submit and then never speak of this to anyone. She would survive this.

The Montagnards were a simple and primitive people. The Vietnamese had stolen their lands, the Central Highlands, some years before, and the Yuan simply took what they wanted from the Montagnards. The Montagnards, or Dega, as they called themselves, had no right to vote, no schools, no hospitals, no representation in government.

They had nothing and even half of that was taken away in taxes and levies by the Vietnamese. They were raped, murdered, pillaged, and plundered by those who held the reins of power in Saigon. The Vietcong treated them the same way. All Vietnamese hated the Montagnards, and the Dega felt the same way toward the Vietnamese.

Nobody could ever figure out why the Vietnamese hated their people so, until their saviors, the American Green Berets, came to live with them. The Americans saw that the primitive Montagnards were a very hard-working, spiritual, family-oriented, loyal, and simple society. On top of that, they were the most aggressive, ferocious fighters in Vietnam. In other words, this aboriginal people who ate rats, bats, monkeys, and everything else that fell to their bamboo crossbows, were everything good that the so-called civilized Vietnamese were not.

Their name for themselves, Dega, meant "Sons of the Mountains," and those jungle-choked, emerald-colored mountains were rich with gold, silver, and other valuable minerals. Besides simple jealousy and fear, the gold was another reason the Vietnamese started killing them off and stealing their lands, beginning in the mid-fifties.

Mua slowly walked toward the river bank as the three Vietnamese soldiers stared at her magnificent body. She proudly lifted her chin and decided not to make a sound or show an emotion. While one pointed his rifle at her, the other two removed their clothes. She said nothing but simply lay down on the grass in the midst of the thicket and spread her legs apart, closing her eyes. They all chuckled evilly and the first entered her and thrust into her violently.

She experienced more pain and fear than anytime in her life, but she would not show anything on her beautiful young face: She was Montagnard. The second entered her and lasted as long as the first. She felt as if a firebrand had been inside her, and she knew true deep hatred for the first time in her fourteen years.

Mua struggled for breath as the third grabbed her by the throat and yanked her into a sitting position. He, too, had removed his clothing and now forced her to take him into her mouth. She provided no satisfaction in that way, so he got between her legs and raped her also.

Not a word was spoken during the entire episode and Mua kept her eyes shut. She lay there listening to the three laughing, talking, and getting dressed. She heard them finally leave, heading for the nearby Special Forces A-camp of Dak Pek.

They went to the LLDB team house and bragged to all the other Vietnamese about their "conquest." At the same time, the young Montagnard girl dived into the cleansing water, her many tears mixing with the swift current. She swam underwater and held her breath until she felt her lungs would explode. If she had an American Green Beret like Ning, he would have killed them and chopped them into little pieces, she thought.

Mua cried in anger, frustration, and rage, but not guilt. She decided that the Vietnamese could make her blood of innocence spill out of her and onto the river-bank, but they could not take her pride or her ability to survive. That was part of being a Montagnard.

She stayed too long for her morning bath, so she put off further tears until she was alone again, and headed for the well-worn trail up to her village gate. Before arriving at the door in the solid wooden, punji-stake-covered wall surrounding the hilltop, Mua knew she had to think of a logical excuse for spending so much time at the river. She had to help her mother prepare meals, thresh rice in the nearby mountain rice fields, and then cut about two hundred pounds of firewood and carry it bundled on her back a half mile to the village.

That night Mua got out of bed, where she had lain crying for an hour. The other single girls sleeping on the woven bamboo matting next to her in the *marao*, the communal stilted longhouse, were all fast asleep and couldn't hear her whispered sobs. Voices had stirred her and she decided to investigate. Mua crept to the wall, where she saw her father, the village chief, speaking to someone on the other side of the wall in Vietnamese. He was the only man in the village who knew the Vietnamese language.

Mua waited, listening to the angry exchange, and then came to her father out of the shadows.

"Father, who was that?" she asked. "What did they want?"

The old man replied, "It was the Vietcong, Mua. He said they would come back tomorrow night, and wanted some rice and meat and some women. If not, they will ambush our villagers when they go to work the rice fields and cut firewood. He said the Americans cannot protect us there."

Mua couldn't help the whimper that escaped her lips, but the old man switched his old M-1 carbine to his other hand and put his sinewy arm around her.

"Mua, don't be afraid," he reassured her. "We will not give anything to the Vietcong. Do not worry."

"We cannot help ourselves with them or the South Vietnamese," she said resignedly. "They are both the same."

"This is very true," he replied. "But the Americans are on the side of the South Vietnamese. That is the only reason the Dega agreed to fight for them. I will get word about this to the Americans. They will help our people."

Mua thought about it. She was excited. The American soldiers were the only ones whom her people could count on, most of the time. Ning's man would know what to do.

She went back to bed and slept fitfully, one time waking up crying.

The young beauty had to force herself to go to the river the next morning, but it was her job to fill up the drinking jugs and wash clothes. She took a quick bath and returned to the village with the water jugs.

Walking up the path to the top of her hill, Mua was puzzled. Above her, several strange Jeh men in traditional loincloths and carrying spears and crossbows entered the village gate. One of the last ones was very tall, and he had a Montagnard woman next to him who was carrying a woven basket, apparently filled with food, on her back.

Oh, well, she thought, maybe it was a peace contingent from Dak Poy across the valley. Their village had been feuding with hers for several years over some silly argument, long since forgotten. Nevertheless she hurried her steps up the path and soon, out of breath, entered the village gate. The strangers were all gathered around her father and all were laughing and talking.

The woman turned and Mua gasped. It was Ning. She was a beautiful woman. She smiled at Mua and then grabbed the arm of her man. Mua stood by the one single tree in the hilltop village and watched with curiosity.

Ning removed her basket and extracted a can of American beer. She smiled at her man as she handed it to him, and he in turn handed the beer to Mua's father. Next, Ning pulled an American "tiger suit" uniform out of her basket and handed that to her man. He put it on over his loincloth and placed an American green beret on his head. Mua got excited. This man wasn't a Montagnard—he was Ning's lover, the American. The man and Ning had come dressed as Jeh, so the VC who saw them from a distance would think they were just an ordinary couple from the village.

The other men were Montagnards, and they reached up under their loincloths and removed rolled-up uniforms that were taped and hidden there. They all dressed, too. They removed the fake bows from the ends of their crossbows, and she saw that they all had rifles that were disguised to look like Montagnard crossbows at a distance.

Ning removed a bunch of metal items from her basket, and Mua watched with awe as the tall American started putting all those parts together. Pretty soon he held an M-16 rifle with a big thick tube on top of it. Mua moved closer.

The American turned his head, noticed the young maiden, and gave her a friendly smile. *Ooh,* she thought, *if I had a man like that, I could have many babies and not fear death from the Yuan for them, or even death from the many diseases that plague my people, or rat bites, snake bites, or even tiger attacks. Such a man would protect me and my children, as he did Ning.*

Ning looked at Mua and flushed. Almost as if Ning could read Mua's mind, she walked over to her man and put her arms around his waist. He stopped looking through the tube device and smiled at the Montagnard beauty. He hugged Ning and gave her a brief but passionate kiss. Mua sighed to herself and caught Ning glancing her way again. Mua blushed and sped away. It was time to get out of sight.

This day, the day after Mua's loss of innocence, turned out to be her most exciting ever. The big American and his friend Nhual, the chief interpreter for Dak Pek, spent the entire day and evening with her father, eating rat, rice, and monkey brains and drinking much rice wine. Mua and her mother got to spend the day watching, as they served meals and cleaned for the warriors. The American checked on Ning several times during the afternoon and always treated her as well as the best Jeh man would treat his woman. Mua wanted the same thing badly.

After dark he left her father's bunker and spoke for a long time with the tough warriors who came with him. Six of them were his bodyguards and were never far away. This man was not only a *Trung-wi,* a first lieutenant, he was also the most important man among the eight thousand Jeh living in the valley and the rest of the Jeh farther south toward Dak To and Kontum.

After the tall *Mil-ken* spoke to the Jeh warriors, they took up positions along the wall around the village. He then sat down by a warm fire and held Ning for a long time. Mua stayed in the shadows and watched as the two touched, laughed, and shared secrets with each other. Mua watched until Ning got sleepy and was taken to the VIP bunker to sleep. Although her father posted two reliable guards outside the bunker door, she saw the *Trung-wi* send two of his bodyguards to watch over his woman. Mua just smiled to herself and hummed.

Next, Nhual and the tall American went to the highest point in the village and lay down with their rifles in their hands. The *Mil-ken* kept looking through the big tube. Earlier in the day, Mua heard it called a "starlight scope," although she could not remember how to say the word. She did ask her father one time what it was, and he explained that it was a magic thing that made the American see at night like an owl. The American could see the VC and shoot them when they could not see him.

Mua was afraid of any look of impropriety on her part, so she went to the *marao* for the single women and went to bed, but she did not sleep a wink all night. She positioned herself against the woven bamboo wall and watched the American long into the night.

After the moon was standing at the very top of the sky, she saw the American carefully looking through the tube and Nhual watching over his sights. Mua then heard the VC call out. They were standing on the outside of the village wall and yelling. Mua heard the confidence, even cockiness, in the VC's voice, even if she could not understand the language. She heard other VC chuckling as the speaker boldy shouted apparent taunts.

The man seemed to be in the middle of a sentence when the American's rifle cracked and spouted flame in the darkness. The voice stopped, and she could tell that the speaker was dead. Mua pretended that it was one of the Yuan who raped her. She smiled broadly in the darkness. Nhual's rifle then cracked and that was followed by another shot by the American. There was a shout by a Vietnamese outside the wall, as he was apparently running toward the nearby jungle when he yelled.

Mua got out of bed, as did the other villagers, and there was, as usual, much running around and confusion until all learned that the American had killed the Vietcong. Ning ran to the tall lieutenant first and kissed him long and hard. Mua sighed.

Her father walked up to the American and Mua heard the man even spoke Jeh. She heard his name as her father spoke. Mua did speak a little bit of French and wondered if the *Mil-ken* might have fought there before with the French, because his name sounded French. He was called *Trung-wi* Bendell.

✳ 3

Know Thy Enemy

I TOOK A TRANSLUCENT plastic cigarette case from the cargo pocket of my jungle fatigues, then pulled out a Lucky, stuck it between my thin lips, and whipped out my Zippo. I looked at the inscription as I lighted the cigarette: 1LT DONALD R. BENDELL, DET A-242 DAK PEK. Below that was the Special Forces crest with the motto DE OPPRESSO LIBER, and below that on the main body of the shiny lighter were inscribed the words: LET ME WIN YOUR HEARTS AND YOUR MINDS OR I WILL BURN DOWN YOUR FUCKING HUT. I looked across the darkened bunker into the black eyes of Mr. Oh, the Jeh Montagnard man seated across the big earthenware crock of rice wine from me. I gave Oh a cigarette, lighted it, and was greeted with a gold-toothed smile.

In my hand was the water-buffalo handle of a Bowie-size knife with a thick blade made from the shrapnel from a 500-pound bomb. It had inscriptions engraved into it from the Jeh tribe of Montagnards. Two small pieces of brass had been ceremoniously inlaid in the back of the blade. One of Mr. Oh's grandchildren held a mouthful of water and, every few seconds, spit a small stream of it on the whetstone I held in my left hand, as I passed the big blade back and forth across the stone. The little copper-skinned naked boy with almond-shaped eyes looked up at me for a wink or smile of approval.

Next to Oh, his wife of twenty years reached up and swatted a pesky fly off her bare brown pendulum breast. She handed me another strip of smoked rat meat. Drying the knife blade on my jungle fatigue pants, I slid it into the bamboo sheath specially sewn into the back of the right thigh part of my trousers. I hid my emotions once more, gulped, put the little strip of meat in my mouth, and chewed.

I couldn't wait for Mr. Oh to pass me the tube extending from the center of the crock. I couldn't wait to fill my mouth with the smooth but deadly rice wine. If I couldn't kill the taste of the rat, maybe I could at least kill some of my brain cells so I could make it through this ordeal without heaving my guts out. During these episodes, I had always been able to make it outside before puking, but there was always a first time, and heaven forbid, I didn't want to insult my host.

At last Mr. Oh finished his long sip of the brew and passed the tube to me. I waited for Mr. Oh's toothless missus to refill the crock with water, and I lifted the tube to my lips. The rat went down okay. Fortunately, I was drunk enough to handle it this time. Lifting the end of the beaded red-yellow-and-blue necklace, I admired it again, then I looked to my right and squarely into the eyes of my Montagnard lover, Ning. As always, her laughing eyes sparkled as she grinned at me, then turned to help Oh's wife wash out the supper bowls.

"Mr. Oh," I said, "this is a beautiful necklace. I really want to thank you and your wife."

Oh's grin faded, and he got deadly serious, "*Trung-uy* Bendell. Americans say *beaucoup* Vietminh—ah—how speak?"

"The Second NVA Division has surrounded Dak Pek," I said, trying to help Oh with his English.

Oh continued, "Maybe we all die now."

"We might," I replied.

The Montagnards had no respect for dishonesty or even beating about the bush.

I thought of the words and remembered arriving in Vietnam in the beginning of June 1968. After processing in through Long Binh, I processed into the Fifth Special Forces Group headquarters in Nha Trang with several other lieutenants from Fort Bragg. We immediately began the COC, or combat orientation course, a three-day affair to let us know what to expect in Vietnam, all the little helpful hints like not wearing after-shave on patrol and faux pas to avoid committing with the indigenous population. The COC concluded with an ambush patrol the last night with Detachment A-502 of Nha Trang.

When the group of newcomers were briefed on the ambush patrol, we were told to take it very seriously.

The NCO instructor said, "Any of you think this is a fucking game, better be aware that one of the guys who just went through this class went out on ambush just last week. He was hiding behind a rice paddy with his ambush patrol and a squad of NVA came by. They sprang the ambush and this lieutenant took an AK-47 round right in his open mouth. It traveled the length of his body. Killed him instantly. He was fighting when it happened, but he still went under. You never know which bullet's yours. Any of you swinging dicks wanna sleep on ambush, remember this ain't no fucking game."

Conscious of the fresh first-lieutenant silver bar on my beret flash, I raised my hand.

"Yes, sir?" the sergeant said, pointing at me.

"Sergeant," I asked, "who was the man that was killed?"

"A first lieutenant, sir, named Roesch," the instructor said, "Heinz Roesch."

A voice startled me into the present.

"Wife, me, and myself," Oh went on, "We have five sons. We make . . . a . . . make promise you. VC come, we fight. First me die, then wife-me die, then five sons-me die, then *Trung-uy* die. VC no come kill, Trung-uy . . . ah . . . must kill family-me first. Necklace is . . . ah . . . necklace is . . . ah . . ."

Clearing my throat, I helped, "Necklace is a symbol, a sign."

Mr. Oh smiled broadly and nodded his head enthusiastically.

He continued, "It is sign of me . . . promise . . . of words-me . . . You friend, Jeh. You friend, family-me."

I rubbed my eyes, "Damn, it's really smoky in your bunker, Mr. Oh."

I ignored the sounds of Ning's and Mrs. Oh's suppressed giggles and continued, "Thank you and your family very much, Mr. Oh. From a man like you this is a great honor. You are my friends."

Oh sat up a little straighter, his chest puffed out.

I went on, "Mr. Oh, the Second NVA surrounded us once before, but they never attacked, so we'll probably survive this too, but if we do get attacked, and I do get killed, you must promise me something else."

"Anyting," the cook said.

I said, "I've made arrangements with FULRO to get Ning into the jungle if I'm ever killed, because she is my woman. Please help with that. Also if I'm killed, please promise that you will make sure the Yards*kill Mr. Bon, the head of the security platoon for the Americans. Tell them to kill his wife, too."

"You know they VC?" Oh replied.

"Yes, I have proof." I continued, "They must be killed. The only way Dak Pek can ever be overrun is with people on the inside."

I sat back and thought about how true my words really were.

Detachment A-242, Dak Pek, was, by the summer of 1968, the most isolated American-manned operation in South Vietnam. Located right in the northwesternmost corner of the II Corps area, it was surrounded by the tallest jungle-covered mountains in South Vietnam. In late 1967, the A-camp directly north of it, Kam Duk, had

* Montagnards

been overrun by the North Vietnamese using Soviet tanks to run interference for their numerous infantry troops.

The A-camp directly south of Dak Pek, Dak Sut, had also been overrun by the NVA prior to that. Dak Seang would be under siege within a few short months. It was the next camp south, and Dak To, to the southeast, had also been overrun shortly before. Directly to the east lay the Tu Mrong Valley, which was one of the strongest NVA strongholds within the borders of Vietnam. Just a few miles to the west lay the Laotian border and the main arteries of the Ho Chi Minh.

The mission of the Special Forces A-team at Dak Pek was to conduct border operations with SF-trained and -equipped Jeh, Sedang, and Halong Montagnards, with a few Cambodians and Laotians mixed in, and interdict North Vietnamese infiltrations into Vietnam from Laos via the Ho Chi Minh Trail.

As isolated as the camp was, however, it was probably the most easily defensible A-camp in South Vietnam. Whoever laid out Dak Pek picked the site well. It was a tactician's dream. Unlike most A-sites, which were in a square, triangle, or some such configuration with a perimeter all the way around, Dak Pek was located on eleven tiny hilltops, each with its own perimeter around it. Each of the eleven hills supported at least two other hills by interlocking direct fire. In other words, if somebody breached the barbed wire, tank trap, punji stakes, and other booby traps surrounding each hill, then small-arms fire, point-blank artillery, recoilless rifles and bazookas, and even flamethrowers could be pointed directly at the backs of the assaulting force from at least two other hills.

On top of that, each hill was ringed by a ten-foot-wide by ten-foot-deep tank trap. Each tank trap was filled with thousands of needle-sharp punji stakes, bamboo stakes sharpened to a point and facing outward. Additionally, the entire perimeter was covered with numerous rolls of triple-strand concertina wire and tanglefoot barbed wire.

All of the Americans stayed on one hill, aptly known as "the American hill," and it had the best defenses. A driveway with a movable barbed-wire gate separated the American hill from the Vietnamese hill.

The rest of the hill was as described, except that an enterprising engineer/demolition specialist from New Jersey, Sergeant Larry Crotsley, added some new features in 1968. With the help of other A-team members and Montagnards, he ringed the hill with fifty-five-gallon drums of aviation jet fuel mixed with several chemicals to form a napalmlike flaming jelly when detonated. These drums were buried on the sides of the hill just below the earth's surface, with electronically detonated charges beneath each drum. The wires ran underground to the Americans' bunkers circling the hill, along with other buried wires to numerous Claymore mines. Each bunker had a series of sketches drawn on a piece of board with the wires attached. The sketch was a crude diagram showing the location and killing zone of each Claymore.

The blacktop runway for aircraft ran through the eastern edge of the camp, outside the main perimeter, but inside the protection of several more outlying hills.

On top of everything else, there were fifty-two World War II vintage .30-caliber machine guns permanently emplaced around the perimeters of each hill, along with seven .50-caliber machine guns, a number of M-60 machine guns, numerous 60-mm and 81-mm and four-deuce mortars, 90 mm and 106-mm recoilless rifles, bazookas, and a 105 howitzer artillery battery on the Vietnamese hill. Every hill was ringed with reinforced bunkers in which lived seven hundred families of armed and trained Montagnard fighters, about the best in Vietnam.

If that were not all, the entire camp was in a giant green jungle valley, all cleared away, and Jeh Montagnard villages with a population of eight thousand covered fifteen other hills surrounding the camp, also providing an early-warning system in case of attack. The clear, cold Dak Poko River flowed through all of this and was joined by the smaller Dak Pek in the south end of the valley. In most places around the camp the two rivers were not fordable.

Dak Pek did have two vulnerabilities: One of those was the fact that it was a sitting duck for indirect-fire weapons because it was surrounded 360 degrees by tall mountains. It was, in fact, the victim of numerous rocket, mortar, and artillery attacks, by both the North Vietnamese Army and occasionally the two companies of ragtag local Vietcong. Most of these were Montagnards from outlying villages who were VC only because the NVA forced them to fight for them or they would kill their families. Consequently, these ill-equipped, unmotivated fighters never posed much of a real threat and were regarded with disdain by the Dak Pek force.

The second weakness was the fact that the Americans had to work with the Vietnamese Special Forces, the *Luc Luong Dac Biet,* or LLDB. Some of the Vietnamese at Dak Pek were Vietcong, that was a given. There was just simply a certain percentage of Vietnamese throughout the country who were VC and there was no way of knowing who they were. The local Montagnard villagers who were members of the Vietcong were generally known by most of the Montagnards in the Dak Pek strike force, but the strikers would never tell the Americans, because they knew that the Yard VC were fighting under duress, not by choice. In many cases, they were relatives—an uncle, cousin, or brother.

The Vietnamese Communist infiltrators in Dak Pek, however, were hard-core, trained intelligence agents. You just could not spot who they were very easily. The head of the Security Platoon that helped guard the American hill, Mr. Bon, was one of these agents. So was his wife. The team intelligence sergeant, Joe Howard, I, and a few others knew this but had yet to prove it. One man who was on the team but was not respected by anyone had actually become friends with Mr. Bon, because he spoke such good English. The man would just open up and talk to him as if he were another American.

Directly to the north of the Dak Pek American team house was a bunker shared by two Green Beret sergeants, and it was the only bunker nobody on the team was allowed into, not even maids. The two NCOs manning the bunker wore green berets and the proper uniform but were not really Special Forces: They were from ASA, the Army Security Agency. Only the team intel sergeant, team commander, team sergeant, and I knew their real function. They had radio equipment inside the bunker that shot directional azimuths on NVA and Vietcong radios operating in the area. Mohawk prop-driven planes would constantly fly around the area loaded with sensitive electronic equipment that also shot directional signals on enemy radio transmissions. These azimuths were computed and intersected and gave them the location of the enemy units. Additionally, the strength of the radio signal told them the size of radio used by each unit, and consequently, the size of the enemy unit. This was how the Americans knew that we were surrounded on all sides by the Second NVA Division.

I attended Vietnamese language school at Fort Bragg before coming to "the big rifle range across the pond" and learned to read, write, and speak a little of the language from Mme. Nhu's sister, who taught, under a different name, at Fort Bragg.

During recent rocket and artillery attacks on Dak Pek, these ASA men had heard a radio operator, inside the camp, adjusting the fire in on the camp. Additionally, this radio operator constantly used a portable telegraph key and usually transmitted right after Commo Willy completed his transmissions on the powerful single-side-band radio. The two ASA men tape-recorded his transmissions, then they and other experts, using computers, would try to break the Communists' code.

They asked me to come to their bunker the next time that Dak Pek came under indirect fire attack and try to translate what the agent within the camp was saying to the North Vietnamese. The other important factor that had happened was the fact that the past several times the agent had transmitted, the ASA people got good azimuths on the radio, and when the azimuths were crossed, the intersection was directly on Mr. Bon's bunker.

A muffled explosion shook the underground bunker and was followed by several more. The sounds brought me out of my thoughts. My hand instinctively went down and my fingers wrapped around my oft-present CAR-15 rifle, which was a sawed-off version of the M-16 with a stock that would telescope by squeezing it and pulling out. Ning jumped under my other arm for protection.

From outside, I heard two American voices shouting, "Incoming! Incoming!"

I pushed Ning into Oh's arms and said, "Stay with them, honey" as I burst out the door.

The bright sunlight hit my eyes like a napalm pie in the face from some giant Soupy Sales. The rice wine I had drunk also hit me and made my knees wobble as I tried to run to the ASA bunker.

I squinted at the concrete block latrine to my left front, and I heard the voice of the team's assistant radio operator, Staff Sergeant Don Williams, known to all as "Commo Willy."

He yelled, "What the fuck!"

The door burst open and the almost-boyish-looking radio operator ran out, pulling up his trousers and a scowl on his face, yelling, "Fucking Commie bastards won't even let a guy take a decent shit around here!"

I chuckled as I watched the youthful-looking staff sergeant disappear down the stairs to the TOC and commo bunker. My chuckles stopped short though when another 220 rocket streaked over my head and crashed into the edge of the runway. The last few yards I half ran, half fell down the steps into the ASA bunker.

Not in any desire of getting shot by friendly fire, I screamed, "American!" right before unceremoniously crashing through the door into their bunker.

I was handed earphones and was treated to a cacophony of guttural Vietnamese vowels and syllables being shouted into the radio inside the camp and out on one of the mountaintops just west of camp.

"What are they saying, sir?" one of the E-6s asked.

I removed one earphone, smiled, and said, "A bunch of scared shit, Sergeant. The guy in camp is scared shitless and is shouting like crazy, and the one out there is excited or pissed, so he's shouting back. I can make out maybe every tenth word. Is it coming from Bon's bunker again?"

The other sergeant replied, "Won't know yet until we have a plane in the area. One's on the way, because we figure he'll be using the key again to give them a BDA report of sorts. He's been transmitting a lot of times after Commo Willy transmits, and he knows we'll be sending in spot reports and an after-action report. We'll nail his little yellow ass then."

Less than a half hour later, one of the ASA NCOs reported that the telegraph key was being used in Bon's bunker. Joe Howard, half the A-Team, and I were summoned to the team commander's bunker. He had been hesitant to do anything that might upset Mr. Bon, who carried weight with the LLDB, in case he wasn't a VC. The CO had finally given in, though, after being pushed by several team members. The men armed themselves to the teeth and headed for Bon's bunker. A new E-5 and I climbed up on top of the bunker and stood on the roof, both armed with sawed-off twelve-gauge pump shotguns loaded with double-aught buck. Joe Howard and another sergeant got outside the far door with M-16s, and Larry

Crotsley, armed with an M-60 machine gun, kicked in the door to Bon's bunker and moved swiftly through the log-and-mud structure, followed closely by the team commander.

As Larry swept through the bunker, screams could be heard from inside, and Bon's wife, the Vietnamese payroll clerk, and several others flooded out the far door, only to be stopped by Howard, myself, and the others. They stood there, hands held high in the air. The bunker was searched thoroughly and someone stated that Bon had gone off to Kontum on a shopping excursion. Mrs. Bon was angry, to say the least, and demanded to know what was going on. The captain tried to explain tactfully that we had a report that a VC was hiding in her bunker, holding her hostage. The radio and telegraph key could not be found.

"Captain," I shouted from the bunker roof, "Bon's wife . . . look at her!"

The captain's face got red and everyone looked in her direction.

"Shut the fuck up, Lieutenant!" he growled.

"Captain," I insisted, "look, she's wearing an *atok!*" That was a Montagnard black full-length wraparound skirt.

"What about it, Bendell?" the captain fumed.

"She's Vietnamese *Dai-uy!*" I screamed, jumping down off the bunker. "The Viets hate the Yards; The Yards hate the Viets! There's no fucking way that a Vietnamese woman would ever wear a Montagnard skirt! Rip her skirt off, Captain! She's got the telegraph key strapped to her thigh!"

Ba Bon got even more angry, but that couldn't touch the anger of the team commander.

He looked at the Vietnamese woman and said, "I'm sorry, Mrs. Bon. Don't pay any attention to the *Trung-uy;* he's *dinky dau.* Too much rice wine."

I was furious, as were Crotsley and Howard.

I said, "Shit, Captain, this fucking bitch is a VC! Let me rip her skirt off, and I'll show you!"

Red-faced, the team commander turned on his heel and stormed off toward the team house with me following.

The captain said, "Bendell, you dumb bastard! When are you going to learn to quit insulting the Vietnamese and making them lose face? Do you know how pissed Mr. Bon is going to be, let alone *Dai-uy* Hoe?"

"Fuck' em!" I said angrily. "Bon's a fucking VC and *Dai-uy* Hoe probably is, too. I know he's getting very rich by running a very lucrative black market here. Let me shoot Bon, and you won't have to worry about how pissed he gets."

The captain stopped and stared, hands on his hips.

Frustrated beyond anger, I threw up my hands, smiled, and said, "Well, I guess you shouldn't be in Special Forces if you can't take a fucking joke."

Shaking my head, I turned and headed for Mr. Oh's bunker to pick up Ning. On the way, I stopped at the team house for a bottle of whiskey. In Special Forces, you had a choice: you either had a sense of humor or you developed one. If not, there wasn't much chance for maintaining sanity, or at the very least avoiding an early coronary. I added to the protection of my mental well-being with alcoholic anesthesia as well.

Commo Willy stumbled out of the dark steps leading from the Tactical Operations Center. The sunlight seemed to have the same effect on the Soupy Sales demon as it had on me. Ning and I laughed at the hungover blond NCO. Commo Willy looked just like the grown-up version of the little boy who stole a piece of pie out of his grandma's window. Green around the gills, however, he now looked as if he had stolen a vat of whiskey from a window. A copy of the *Army Times* in his hand, he was apparently returning to the seat he had already warmed up in the latrine.

"Hi, Ning," he said. "Lieutenant, did we have a rice wine celebration last night or what?"

"Hell, if I know," I replied, "I don't remember yesterday."

Ning giggled, "We have big camp celebration. You both drink *beaucoup* rice wine."

"Man, this morning I woke up and there was a bowl of these swollen round things by my bed. I about puked. I still feel sick," the sergeant said. "You know what they looked like? Miniature assholes."

"Miniature assholes?" I said and started laughing.

Ning laughed again and said, "You fix Cheerios and milk last night. You eat."

"You mean that was Cheerios and milk by my bed?" He walked on to the latrine, mumbling, "Man, it looked like miniature assholes."

Ning giggled heartily while I, wearing a grin stolen from the lower half of Sonny Bono's face, watched him walk away. We went to my bunker and disappeared into the eye-saving darkness.

My bunker was small; in fact, it was downright claustrophobic and was divided by a plywood wall into two rooms. Joe Howard occupied the left and I the right. The bunker had dirt walls and was underneath a sandbagged .50-caliber machine gun emplacement. The six dirt steps down into the bunker ran off the sides of a 4.2-inch mortar bunker.

I switched on the light and flopped down on my bed, still fuming. The light went off and I turned around, staring at the beautiful Montagnard woman. She had removed her *atok* and was wearing only a beaded leather thong that wrapped around her hips and dipped down above the sparse triangle of black hair that formed the apex of her beautiful symmetrical body. Her shiny black hair hung over one shoulder and tickled my face when she hovered over it.

Husky-voiced, she said, "Maybe tomorrow VC kill.

Maybe we die. Today is not tomorrow. Today we live, but we go heaven."

Her lips closed around mine and our bodies melted into each other. Somebody outside the bunker decided to fire harassing-and-interdictory—H-and-I—fires with the four-deuce mortar. The bunker thundered as rounds were dropped and shot out of the tube with loud metallic thumps. Round after round was fired and the power could be felt by the vibrations in the bunker.

The head cook for the Special Forces A-team at Dak Pek went by one name and one name only, Hazel. Vietnamese, she had many expensive negligees and ladies' undergarments. She had been the madam of a successful brothel in Kontum before coming to Dak Pek.

The woman did have a few problems. One was her voice. It sounded as if, one night when Hazel was sleeping, some leprechauns sneaked in, removed her larynx, ran it along a gravel road for about twenty miles, then sneaked back and replaced it before she awakened.

There was another thing about her, too. The way she made herself up. Well, at some time, Tammy Faye Bakker apparently saw some pictures of Hazel somewhere and said, "I want my makeup to look just like hers."

Hazel was always friendly, though. In fact, with some of the guys on the team, she was exceptionally friendly at night, after the kitchen was closed and the sun was hiding somewhere beyond the horizon, recharging its batteries so it could broil some more hapless victims the next day.

Her cooking was really good, too. Everyone liked Hazel. Everyone liked Hazel's cooking. The guys who knew her before she came to Dak Pek even liked her whorehouse in Kontum too.

That was the big problem. Those who just wanted to come to Dak Pek, do their job for one year, and get back to "the World," never stopped and thought or asked, "Why?"

Why would an aging whorehouse madam with a lucrative business in a city come to the most isolated American outpost in Vietnam? As much as the Vietnamese hated and despised the Montagnards, why would a successful "woman in the business," who was Vietnamese, come and live among the Montagnards, and one of the most primitive tribes at that? Why would such a woman choose to live in a six-by-eight-foot underground bunker, especially in an area where she was surrounded by man-eating tigers, football-size rats, bamboo vipers, spitting cobras, banded kraits, malaria-carrying anopheles mosquitoes, and the Second NVA Division? Hazel tried to screw just about every team commander at Dak Pek. She tried to screw intel sergeants and radio operators, too, but she never tried to screw assistant medics or light-weapons men, or anyone who was not working all day with the type of intel that the NVA needed. Not enough people stopped and asked themselves, "Why was she there?"

A good warrior will keep his weapon clean. He will break it down and check it for dirt and mud and rust. Some guys boiled a big tub of water, put all the parts of their weapon in it, and cleaned it with a brush while it was underwater. They quickly dried it and went over the whole thing with solvent. Some gave it a coat of oil and carefully rubbed it off. Some worked over the stock and any wooden parts with linseed oil, even furniture polish. They ran cotton swabs down the barrel over and over until they could sight down the inside of the barrel with a cleaning patch being held in the chamber with light shining on it. The barrel couldn't show anything but shine and rifling grooves. Warriors who took that much care with their weapons, more often than not, lived to fight many battles.

Every night with towel and soap, oils and creams, makeup and toiletries, Hazel headed for the shower room.

The following day, the 403rd ASA still picked up

readings of an entire division of NVA in the mountains surrounding Dak Pek. The men of the team slept even more lightly. In fact, each was awakened constantly by sounds such as flea farts. And so it was, that the Green Berets required sledgehammers to insert pins into their rectums for a period of time thereafter.

On the fourth day after the initial report, an excited villager from one of the outlying Jeh villages rushed through the sandbagged front gate of Dak Pek. He scurried up the hill to the American team house and looked for a Jeh interpreter to speak with, not being comfortable talking directly to one of the big Americans. He held in his hand an eight-by-ten sheet of yellow paper with black printing on it.

Suet, a fifteen-year-old interpreter with a wife and two children, read the paper and spoke with the villager and sent for me and a couple other team members. Suet had been hired by the Americans because he had got into a fight with a Vietnamese when only thirteen years of age. The stocky bronze-skinned young man killed the fully grown Vietnamese with his bare hands. This was just too much for the macho soldiers, so they rewarded the young Montagnard warrior by hiring him with the best paying, most prestigious job in the camp: interpreter for the Americans. Then they set about teaching him to speak English.

Two sergeants and I looked at the document while we were told that several local Vietcong had come up to the village gate the previous night and nailed that paper and several identical to it to the gate and then left. I couldn't let anyone see anything but my macho mask, but I felt the bottom drop out of my stomach as I read the printed leaflet. It stated that Lieutenant Donald R. Bendell would be assassinated between the hours of twelve noon the next day and twelve noon the day following. The paper had been printed on a printing press.

The first thing I noticed was that the paper had no

nail holes in it, and the second thing I noticed was that the man who brought it in was the son of the village chief for Dak Long Hnang. That village was the one who supplied the most fighters for the local Vietcong. In fact, every male member of Dak Long Hnang was a VC, including the man excitedly showing the paper to us. Suet and I both knew this.

In a false show of bravado, I rolled the printed paper up, stuck a Swisher Sweet cigarillo in my mouth, lighted the paper, and used it to light the cigar.

I said to Suet, "Tell him to ask his father if I may visit with him and sleep in his village tonight."

"Trung-uy Bendell," Suet said, "his village is VC. They kill you."

"I don't think so," I said, "I think Dak Long Hnang might be the safest place for me to sleep tonight."

Suet translated and the man promised to return to his village and come back with an immediate answer.

As we walked into the team house, one of the sergeants, a blond-haired E-5 who had been a surfer growing up in Malibu said, "Man, I think you're fucking crazy, sir. No American has ever stayed overnight in that village. Everyone knows that they're fuckin' VC sympathizers."

"And they're trying to terrorize us, Sergeant," I answered. "What better way to show them that their propaganda won't work, if we eat, drink, then lay down and sleep with the enemy, on their own turf?"

"Still think it's fucking goofy."

Later that afternoon, a contingent of tiger-suited CIDG strikers from Dak Pek and I entered the wooden door of the punji-covered wall surrounding the hilltop village of Dak Long Hnang. Nhual, the head interpreter from the A-camp and my best friend, accompanied the small patrol. The village chief greeted us at the gate and escorted us around his filthy village, proudly showing it off. Clad in a black loincloth, he showed more of his dirty old balls than he did of his village defenses.

After seeing the village, I said, *"Ba Nua"*—my term of close friendship, which meant "Father of Nua"—"tell him that I am honored to be his guest and am impressed with this dirty piece of shit."

Nhual chuckled and I continued, "Tell him that I will make sure a MEDCAP comes out this week."

As the stocky Jeh man with the red-streaked hair and intelligent eyes translated and edited my comments, the old village chief just beamed. The villagers were always happy to receive the medical civic action patrols, because the American medics treated the villagers for a variety of maladies, in addition to which the people were given free soap, clothing sent from churches, and other goodies.

I walked along with Nhual and the village chief, shadowed by the six Montagnard bodyguards who accompanied me everywhere.

Nhual spoke. "Don, did you see how excited he got over the MEDCAP?"

I replied, "Yeah, it's funny, *Ba Nua*. In my country, there are antiwar protesters running around yelling because they think we are raping Vietnamese women and killing their babies and shooting their poor husbands in black pajamas with rusty old rifles."

Nhual slapped his palm to his forehead, "Last month a Soviet bomber flies over Dak Pek. Last week NVA fly into our area in Soviet helicopters. The NVA's weapons are much better in the jungle than ours. I have an M-16, but all the strikers use weapons that Americans used in World War Two! I guess some Americans are not primitive like my people, but are just dumb, huh?"

He looked at me for a reaction.

I laughed. "Amen to that, brother. They don't mention the schools, churches, or hospitals we build or things like that, especially Special Forces."

"Why?" Nhual queried.

"Beats the shit out of me," I went on. "Since the

President picks out bombing targets and won't let the generals run this cluster-fuck they call a war, that may have something to do with it."

"What will happen to us when you all leave?" Nhual asked.

"You know the answer to that," I said, lighting a cigar.

We entered the village chief's bunker and sat down at a crock of rice wine, which had been fermenting for just such an occasion. The wrinkled old man held a tube across the earthen jar and I smiled, nodded, and put it to my lips.

A weathered old woman poured dirty water into the big crock as the chief grinned and said, *"My huit nhiaa."*

I grinned and said, *"Au wa huit nhiaa. Liem jai!"*

With that I took a long sip from the crock of potent alcohol and watched the water level below the bamboo stick that pointed down into the crock. When doing some serious drinking, which was the only way they drank, the Jeh drank "sticks." Pouring water into the potent wine, they raised the level of the liquid to the top of the big crock. The drinker then drank until the liquor went below a bamboo stick that protruded downward from another stick across the top of the crock. The water made the rice swell, raising the wine level continuously, so drinking slowly meant you drank more wine. If the drinker removed the drinking tube from his lips before getting the level of fluid below the stick, the crock would be filled again with more water. The only way to drink sticks was to siphon wine into your gut as quickly as possible, so you still got blasted.

I drank a stick and handed the tube to the village chief, who attached himself like a baby at the nipple. Mrs. Chief handed me a bowl with some shredded, boiled bamboo and pieces of rat and monkey, cooked together. I ate while the village chief drank of the potent potable.

I finished my meal and set the bowl down, lighted a

Lucky, and offered one to the glassy-eyed chief, who had just finished his primitive brewski.

"Nhual," I said calmly while lighting the old man's cigarette, "tell him I know he is VC, along with all of his relatives."

Nhual grinned and translated. The man choked on the cigarette and his hand went to the old M-1 carbine lying nearby. His hand froze on the old rifle, however, as he heard the cocking of the Smith and Wesson .357 magnum and stared down the barrel of it. His eyes followed the line of the barrel up my right arm to my grinning face. I holstered the gun, and only then did the chief, Nhual, and I notice one of his bodyguards uncocking his own M-2 carbine while squatting in the doorway of the village chief's bunker.

I said, "Tell him I know why his village is VC. I understand."

Nhual translated and the man smiled.

I went on as Nhual translated, "You must do what you have to to protect your family, but never let the NVA order you to try to kill the people at my camp. Then we will have to kill you and your people."

The man bowed his head and listened, a grave look on his face, and nodded his understanding.

I went on, "If the NVA order you to do something to us or find out something about us, you must come and tell me, and we will work it out. If I am not there, tell Sergeant Joe Howard. You can trust him."

The man finally spoke and Nhual translated his words, "I know you are the head of the FULRO for our tribe. Sometimes we think the FULRO forgets us because we are not Rade, Jarai, Bahnar, or Kaho. We are the lowly Jeh and the Vietnamese try to help the bad spirits in the jungle to kill us off, but you try to help my people. Your heart is good. You are welcome and safe in my village, but the Communists might try to come and kill you while you are here. I know they will."

I smiled. "I know you cannot fight them, and if we protect you, they will come at night when we are not here, but there are ways, old man. When will the bastards come to you again?"

"Probably tonight," the old man said, "to kill you."

I smiled again and said through Nhual, "Good. Tell them I came out to tell you to tell them that we are going to send out operations to find those who printed that message. The NVA have said that they will pay one million piasters to anyone who kills me, but everyone knows that they only pay with IOUs that are worthless. Tell them and tell everyone in the valley that I will pay five hundred dollars—translate that into piasters—out of my own money, for the head of any NVA or VC who prints leaflets or puts bounties on Americans. Tell him that we will start cutting the heads, fingers, and penises off of every VC or NVA we kill. That'll get them, *Ba Nua,* if they are the right religion."

Nhual grinned and said, "Many of them will wonder if their soul will escape from their body and wander forever."

I grinned also and said, "That's the message we want to get across."

Nhual translated and the man smiled and spoke. "You will be safe here tonight. All fear your bodyguards —they are the best Jeh fighters in the valley. Our men will die before you die. I will die first. You will be safe here."

I smiled and said to Nhual, "Don't tell him that I said if he wasn't such a pussy and would have stood up to the NVA to begin with, we wouldn't have any of this to worry about. Tell him I said that the Jeh are not lowly. They are the greatest fighters of all thirty-one tribes. I feel honored and safe to stay in his village tonight. Between us, I'll lay here, but I'll really sleep back at camp tomorrow. Feed him any other bullshit you think will help."

"No sweat," Nhual replied. "We will all be awake tonight. I will tell you something. He does not want to fuck with the FULRO."

The *Front de Liberation de Hauts Plateaux-Montagnards,* or FLHPM, was a Montagnard resistance movement comprised of members of all thirty-one tribes from the primitive mountain people in Vietnam's Central Highlands region. Their goal was to regain the autonomy given to them by the French with an ordinance dated May 27, 1946, and again recognized by the last king of Vietnam, Bao Dai. The first president, however, Ngo Dinh Diem, in 1955 ignored the Montagnards' independence and started moving Vietnamese from the lowlands along the coast and the southern Delta region up into the Central Highlands in the Montagnard population centers. The FLHPM wanted the Montagnards' country, the Central Highlands, back and was willing to fight for it. Additionally, they wanted the Vietnamese to stop the years of discrimination against the Montagnards. They were regularly killed, had no schools, churches, or hospitals, no right to vote, or even representation in government. Finally, because of US pressure during the war, the Saigon government created an Office of Ethnic Minority, which was actually a "paper tiger" to appease the Americans.

The FLHPM was a descendant of the 1958-founded resistance movement called the BAJARAKA, the latter an acronym formed from the first two letters of the names of the top four tribes: the Bahnar, Jarai, Rade, and Kaho. It was headed by a charismatic Rade named Y-Bham Enuol. Y-Bham also headed a trilateral resistance movement comprised of the FLHPM, along with the Cambodian Khmer Krom resistance called the FLHPKN or *Front de Liberation de Hauts Plateaux-Kambuja Nord* and the Cham people's resistance called the FLHPC, or *Front de Liberation de Hauts Plateaux-Champa.* This trilateral front was known as the *Front de Lutte de Races-Opprime,* or FULRO.

The few Americans who knew about these resistance movements primarily called the Montagnard resistance movement the FULRO. This was probably due to the fact that Um Savath and Les Kosem, who headed the other two respective movements, kind of suckered Y-Bham into the trilateral front because they wanted to use the tremendous war power the fierce and dedicated Montagnard fighters could provide to achieve their own ends. Special Forces personnel were warned to stay away from the FULRO, because Saigon was our ally, and we were not to get involved in the internal problems of their country. Most SFers who got very close with the Yards, however, could not help getting involved in their plight when they saw how poorly they were treated by the Vietnamese. Many SF people did secretly get involved with the FULRO through wanting to see the Yards, who were very loyal and staunch allies, at least get an even break.

In fact, in 1964, the FULRO pulled off a coordinated rebellion in five Special Forces camps and the city of Ban Me Thuot. They carefully put American Green Berets under armed guards in their team houses while they hanged Vietnamese from flagpoles, dumped them in latrine seats, and machine-gunned them to death. They even took over the Ban Me Thuot radio station and intended to broadcast the rebellion to all the Yards in the Central Highlands to get them to take up arms, but the people were so primitive and uneducated they couldn't find anyone who knew how to operate the transmitter, so they gave up on that idea.

I had personally been commissioned by Y-Bham Enuol as commander of the Jeh in the FULRO, and after that six Jeh bodyguards followed me everywhere, watching over me constantly—sometimes from a distance, but they were always there. The FULRO was supported by all Montagnards and its leaders cut a wide swath among the people. The FULRO was, and is, with the Montagnards essentially what would have happened with the Native Americans, years ago, had the Iroquois, Apache, Sioux, Cherokee, Cheyenne, Navajo, Arapaho, Mohawk and all the other tribes set aside their tribal differences and languages and formed a secret movement to fight against the white man.

Many rumors, over the years, have stated that the CIA secretly supplied arms and equipment to the FULRO, but that has never been proved. Any Americans with the FULRO would certainly never confirm that, and the Montagnards wouldn't want to bite any hands that might have possibly fed them.

The next night, the psychological operations people from the Second NVA Division set up loudspeakers on a mountain west of Dak Pek. In Vietnamese they blasted a message to the eight thousand Montagnards and ten or twelve Americans in the valley of the Dak Poko. They said that Dak Pek was surrounded, and they were going to invade the camp and kill everyone: men, women, and children. There was one way to avoid this, however: simply capture the American Green Berets and tie them up. The NVA would then peacefully walk into Dak Pek and everybody would live happily ever after. Fortunately, the Montagnards had been lied to so many times by the Vietnamese, both North and South, they didn't even give the propaganda promises a moment's thought.

Promises and IOUs were one thing, but ass-kicking was another thing altogether. The American members of Dak Pek who had been around the ARVN, the Army of the Republic of Vietnam, didn't have much respect for their fighting prowess. The Green Berets did, however, respect the people they fought from the Second NVA Division. They firmly believed that no pussies slept in their foxholes, except for the women who wore uniforms and shot as well as the men and boys.

4

Feints and Haymakers

THE SECOND NVA DIVISION moved out of the mountains ringing Dak Pek, and a month later elements of the Second NVA Division—more specifically, the 24th NVA Regiment—hit Dak Seang, the next camp south. Wounded, the former weapons NCO from Dak Pek, Chuck Challela, and the team commander, Captain Jimmy Chiles, rallied the Dak Seang force along with other team members and repelled the attack. At dawn of the first morning, numerous bodies of NVA sappers lay everywhere in the barbed wire of Dak Seang. The siege of the camp lasted for weeks, but they were finally driven away, temporarily.

Elements from Dak Pek, led by me, along with a buck sergeant, Lawrence Vosen, came to Dak Seang along with the Kontum Mike Force led by Captain Joe Dietrich who ended up as team commander at Dak Pek, and another force came from Mang Buk. Another group of Yards from Dak Seang led by Chuck Challela all combined to fight the 24th NVA and kicked their butts into Laos. The next time Dak Seang got hit, however, the camp was overrun and remained in NVA possession.

Dak Pek got surrounded again by the Second NVA Division. This time an operation from Dak Pek did get overrun in the middle of the night. Big Larry Crotsley, the engineer/demolition specialist, and Joe Howard, the dark-haired thin Texan who was the team intel sergeant, were out in the mountains due east of Dak Pek. They were in command of Dak Pek's recon platoon, which was a misnomer. The recon platoon was actually comprised of two platoons of the best Jeh warriors in Dak Pek's fighting force. They were headed by one platoon leader who was essentially more of a company commander. Incidentally, every man in the recon platoon, as it was called, was also a member of the FULRO.

The unit had searched an area between the A-camp and the NVA stronghold known as the Tu Mrong Valley, which was on the other side of the big mountain range due east of the camp. The unit had been out for maybe a week and was headed back close to the base, when the A-camp came alive, in the middle of the night, to the sounds of small-arms fire and numerous explosions. The alarm was sounded and everyone was out of bed and in defensive positions on the A-camp's perimeter within minutes. That night the strikers, Americans, and Viets within the camp were treated to sights and sounds that haunted and entranced them at the same time.

Less than twenty-four hours earlier, intelligence reports from the 403rd ASA verified that the Second NVA Division had again surrounded the little camp. It was quite obvious, too, that a large element of the division had also surrounded the small unit east of the camp. The unit was on its way back to Dak Pek to beef up its capabilities.

Their position was only several clicks, or kilometers, outside the camp, but there is no way for the average person to understand how far that can be. In New York City, the distance to the recon platoon could be walked to and back during a person's lunch hour. In the American West, a rancher's wife could watch her husband trot his horse that distance in a short period of time, turn around, and trot back, and his horse would hardly be breathing hard.

In the mountains outside Dak Pek, however, it was a different matter. Dak Pek was surrounded by the tallest and steepest mountains in all of Vietnam, and it was surrounded by the thickest jungle. Most fire fights with North Vietnamese Army units and the Special-Forces-led mercenaries took place at distances sometimes only ten feet apart. Even then, many times, the jungle was so thick that the enemy forces couldn't even see each other. The steaming ground was thick, black, and covered with green tanglefoot and vines that had not seen daylight in hundreds of years, in some cases. The triple-canopy jungle above let only tiny slivers of sunlight through as frequently as rain leaks in the Astrodome. When trying to traverse this wild tropical rain forest, you cross numerous creeks and rivers that cannot be seen by aerial reconnaissance. There are hills and mountains there that seem to have slopes straight up and down and are covered with a constant wet mud under the thick green leech-filled carpet. To climb these slopes, you literally have to chop or force the many branches, vines, and leaves to the side, pull on trees and branches while climbing up, and then use the bases of trees almost like ladder rungs. With the muddy footing, you usually climb up ten feet and then slide back down twenty and start over again. You could be on the side of a mountain, in full view of those in the camp, but still be hours of weary hiking away from the camp itself. Such was the case the night that the recon platoon got hit.

Crotsley and Howard had their forty-some Yards set up a perimeter on a small hill running off a ridge of a high mountain within sight of Dak Pek. The wiry little warriors dug defensive positions in the jungle floor, and Joe and Larry strung up their jungle hammocks on each side of the perimeter.

When an SF man on an operation in that area bedded down for the night, there were some fairly standard practices with different variations for each man. Most guys made an overhanging roof with an army poncho tied between two trees with suspension line and the corners tied out to other trees. Under that, a jungle hammock was usually stretched tight. Next the American normally stuck a forked stick in the ground and hung his weapon and ammo harness within easy arm's reach of the hammock. The pack was normally placed on the ground directly underneath the hammock, and last, he would stick two sticks in the ground and place his jungle boots over them upside down to dry out and to prevent poisonous bugs or step-and-a-halfs from crawling inside.

A step-and-a-half was the American slang term for the bamboo viper, one very deadly snake. They abounded in the area around Dak Pek and were responsible for more than one death. They got their name because of the neurohemotoxic poison they emitted with their bite. It was so powerful and fast-acting that soldiers joked that if bitten, you could take only a step and a half before you died. Medics regularly warned soldiers that the best first aid for a bite from a step-and-a-half was to light up a cigarette and enjoy as much of it as possible before you expired. Fortunately, they didn't have fangs like a rattler, copperhead, or cottonmouth, but had rows of teeth and had to chew on the victim like a coral snake. Their bite, however, affected the nervous system like the bite of a coral snake, but it also affected the bloodstream like the bite of a rattler, copperhead, or cottonmouth.

Joe and Larry put out their LPs, checked on their perimeter, made sure defensive plans were coordinated, and then settled in for the night. They both started to sleep a little more soundly than usual, because they had only the recon platoon Montagnards with them and weren't saddled with the usual problems and upsets of having the LLDB, the Vietnamese Special Forces, counterparts with the operation. Actually, the Americans usually referred to them as the LLVC.

Larry Crotsley was probably very glad to get away from the Vietnamese in the camp for a while, because he certainly had his share of problems with them of late. Besides the constant turmoil the LLDB caused by trying to upset the Americans or make them "lose face," the Vietnamese at Dak Pek, for some odd reason, had not long before, started pulling a prank that the Americans didn't appreciate. Stupidly, Vietnamese picked Larry Crotsley, far and away the largest and strongest guy on the team, for the brunt of these pranks. The Vietnamese would walk by an unsuspecting victim and suddenly reach over and squeeze his groin. This usually made the victim jump with fright and all howled with laughter. It also became a technique for them to try to make Americans lose face.

One hot afternoon Larry Crotsley walked down the driveway from the American hill and Mr. Ho, the camp schoolteacher, and another Vietnamese walked toward him up the driveway. Suddenly, laughing, Mr. Ho reached out and grabbed Larry's balls and gave them a squeeze. The two men really didn't have time to laugh, because Larry Crotsley grabbed the Vietnamese clown by the hair and uppercutted him in the gut so hard, it lifted the man at least two feet straight up in the air. Ho came down like a bag of wet cement, spilling its thick, wet contents all over the driveway.

The next day Larry and another sergeant went to the arms room, next to the Americans' shower room, to check with the Montagnard there who was repairing a war trophy of Larry's. Two Vietnamese were in the small bunker in front of the workbench, which was piled high with carbine barrels. One grinned, reached out, and tweaked Larry's balls. Will they never learn? Larry grabbed the hair on the back of the man's head and slammed his face into the pile of barrels, knocking him out cold. The sergeant stepped across the Vietnamese and calmly walked away with the other American.

That night Mr. Ho, totally drunk, showed up in the doorway of the American team house, where the assembled Americans and some Montagnards were watching a motion picture in sixteen millimeter. He held a high explosive hand grenade in each hand, the pins pulled. Everyone just stared as he stepped inside holding up the two grenades.

Thick-tongued, he slurred in broken English, "You Americans make me lose face. Now we all die together."

Nhual said sarcastically, "Go away, you drunken coward, before somebody kicks your ass."

Oddly enough, the man swayed in the doorway for a few minutes and then walked away. Nobody even followed him. No explosions were heard afterward either. The movie was good.

In the wee morning hours, the camp alert was given as a battalion of North Vietnamese hit the two Americans and forty-some Jeh warriors from the north, east, and west sides of their perimeter. They didn't probe. They didn't toss rocks at the automatic weapons positions to get them to fire and pinpoint them. They just swarmed en masse over the allied position. Montagnards tried to return fire, but it was forty-plus men with World War II weapons against over five hundred trained, uniformed, well-equipped soldiers. The Dak Pek strikers just fled into the jungle in forty different directions and tried to fight their way between NVA soldiers.

Larry Crotsley and Joe Howard had wisely already discussed a rendezvous point in case of such an event and both reached there with their interpereter in less than half an hour. That was how long it took for Puff to arrive.

"Spooky" or "Puff, the Magic Dragon" was the Stealth bomber of the Vietnam War. An upgraded World War II vintage C-47 prop plane, it was equipped with four computer-guided electronic Gatling guns that fired eight thousand rounds of 7.62 mm ammunition per minute. The computer locked each gun on a target, then held the firing on it while the plane continued to fly.

It was rumored that a Spooky was capable of covering every square foot of a football field with bullets in less than one minute of firing. Every fourth round from the Gatling guns was a tracer. Consequently, when watching a Spooky firing at night it looked, at a distance, as if there was a ribbon of flame shooting out of it and waving down into the ground.

Joe Howard and Larry rendezvoused at the place they had preplanned and several Montagnards were with them. The rest had vanished into the black enemy-filled jungle. Joe Howard spoke with the FAC (forward air controller) as those in the camp heard the drone of the C-47 engines when the old plane entered the skies over the Valley of Dak Pek. Joe's radio call sign was "Kansas Oxfly Alpha" and the FAC's was "Bird Dog Two-oh." The FAC had flown in from Dak To, arriving minutes before the Spooky.

The men of the team sat around the AN/PRC-25 radio in the team house listening to the conversation on the ground-to-air frequency.

"Kansas Oxfly Alpha, Bird Dog Two-oh, over."

"Bird Dog Two-oh, you got Oxfly Alpha, over."

"Alpha, Two-oh. Heard you need some help getting some people off your back. Got a Spooky here with me. Over."

"Big Rog, I got an eyeball on him and we can use the help, over."

Suddenly an antiaircraft position opened up with fire at Spooky from the big mountain at the south end of the valley. Tracers fired up into the sky and flared out thousands of feet up. The people at Dak Pek watched with openmouthed wonder as the drama unfolded.

"Alpha, Two-oh, stand by, got a little problem, over."

"Standing by, out."

The Spooky banked sharply and circled back toward the antiaircraft position, as those on the ground wondered if the big ship was going to get shot down by the 57 mike-mike. Everyone watched the blinking lights and most felt the aircraft was dangerously low, and all of a sudden, the noise was there but the plane disappeared. At least, its lights had anyway.

Now it was a new ball game. The men of Detachment A-242 laughed and slapped each other on the back, as they saw the lights suddenly come on from Spooky. As quickly, the lights went out and a trail of tracers shot up into the black sky. From another part of the sky a long slowly waving ribbon of flame suddenly appeared and went down into the mountainside where the antiaircraft fire had originated. The sheet of flame was followed, seconds later, by the staccato sound of the Gatling guns, which sounded something like a distant symphony from jackhammers being operated simultaneously. The lights came back on in the circling plane and went out again, but this time there was no more antiaircraft fire. The Spooky turned his lights on and headed for Larry and Joe's position.

"Oxfly Alpha, this is Bird Dog Two-oh. You still with me? Over"

"Two-oh, this is Alpha. We're here, but it's getting hot. Over."

"No problem, Alpha, how about marking your position with a flare. Over."

Larry Crotsley fired a red parachute flare up into the night sky. The team members heard the murmur of several nearby Montagnards as they looked at the pyrotechnic device hanging lazily above the nearby jungle. Suddenly, though, a short distance north, another red parachute flare popped and also hung suspended above the eerie scene.

"This is Two-oh, Alpha. I see two red flares. Over."

Joe apparently couldn't see the enemy's flare and the surprise was evident in Joe's voice.

"Two flares. We only shot one. Over."

"Charlie's imitating you. Send me up another one. Over."

The men watching from the team house were

amazed as they watched another parachute flare being shot into the sky, followed by another, a short distance to the north. Both of these flares were green. The NVA were obviously very well equipped. It was a common practice for the NVA to monitor America's radios, so if a man sent out a smoke or a flare for an aircraft and told the aircraft what color, then Charlie just put out the same color of smoke or flare.

The safe procedure was to send up a smoke or a flare, then have the pilot say, "I see red," "green," or whatever.

These NVA were actually watching Larry and Joe's flares, probably with several people ready to launch a hand-held flare of a matching color. As soon as Larry and Joe's flare appeared, the NVA fired one of the same color.

"I see two green flares. Shoot up another. I'm coming down on the deck for a closer look. Over."

Larry fired another red flare up through the jungle canopy. A second later another red flare illuminated the sky a little to the north of Larry's. The little single-engine 0-1 plane dipped down close to both flares and and several tracer rounds shot up at it from the jungle below the northernmost flare. The plane flew quickly out over the A-camp.

"Alpha, this is Two-oh. I got two red flares, but I assume that's not you shooting at me. Over."

"Roger. Over."

"I didn't think so. Nice of them to mark their position for me. Get your heads down. Over."

"Roger, out."

A sheet of flame shot down out of the Spooky circling high up in the night sky. The bright ribbon churned into the triple-canopy jungle and the staccato sounds of the modern guns followed. The ribbon disappeared and the plane kept circling. The ribbon streaked out of its side again and the triple-canopy jungle below was quickly and violently defoliated. This went on for some time, then Spooky suddenly broke off, flying toward the south.

"Oxfly Alpha, Two-oh, think we did you any good? Over."

"That's a big Rog, Two-oh. You definitely put a hurtin' on 'em. Thanks. We heard some secondaries and some screaming, too. Over."

"Sounds good, Alpha. I'll be back at first light. Anything comes up in the meantime, give me a shout, Bird Dog Two-oh, I'm out of here. Out."

Larry and Joe gathered their handful of Montagnards and formed a little defensive perimeter, waiting for daylight. There was sporadic fire and explosions throughout the rest of the night. Every once in a while another Montagnard appeared at the rendezvous point, but by daylight over thirty of the tough Jeh warriors were still missing.

After daybreak, the two Americans led their little patrol to the NVA position of the previous night. The recon platoon's perimeter that had been overrun was covered with chewed-up bodies of North Vietnamese soldiers. The entire area was just one mass of destruction from the thousands and thousands of bullets. Four of the dead NVA soldiers were women. All were in new uniforms with name tags and insignia.

The patrol was ordered to return to the camp. Joe and Larry arrived within a few hours. Plans were made to launch a bigger operation to go out and look for the missing Montagnards. In the midafternoon, however, numerous people started yelling. Soon the whole camp was alerted and looked to the edge of the jungle to the east of the camp. Amid cheers from virtually every man, woman, and child in Dak Pek, a long file of Jeh warriors marched out of the jungle, headed toward the A-camp of Dak Pek. Some of the men had pieces of cloth wrapped around various wounds. Some had no clothing and wore only a loincloth, as they had been overrun just as they were changing clothes. At least ten of them had lost their rifles and carried handmade spears. One proudly carried his M-2 carbine at port arms. The entire stock was missing, though, and the man's T-shirt was wrapped around his hand, where an AK-47 bullet had gone through his hand and the rifle stock, too, but his life was spared.

Several Dak Pek NCOs ran to the refrigerator and grabbed cans of Budwesier beer. The team commander told Hazel to make steak and potatoes for every one of the strikers. An escort hopped into a jeep and ran down the hill to meet the patrol as they crossed the Dak Poko River and marched directly to the American team house, led by the head of the recon platoon.

At the team house they were enthusiastically greeted and congratulated by all of the American team members. They had beer and steak dinners, then each man was given a black neckerchief with the words DAK PEK STRIKE FORCE embroidered on the back. Several seamstresses in Kontum had been recently hired to make the scarves, which were also worn by all the team members, with the plans to give a scarf to any striker who performed heroically in battle. It was a badge of honor.

Incredibly, the wily Jeh were able to hide during the night all over the jungle-covered mountain and located each other by midday. Of the forty-some men that Joe Howard and Larry Crotsley took on the operation, a number were slightly wounded, but every single man made it back to Dak Pek alive.

The North Vietnamese Army was tough and dedicated. A few months earlier, another lieutenant was commanding an operation on a mountaintop fire support base just east of Ben Het, the second camp south of Dak Pek. He was captured by a unit from the Second NVA Division that overran his FSB. The lieutenant who was wounded and captured was Lieutenant Leopold, whom I saw staring into space in the truck when he and I were in training.

They attacked full-out one night while Leopold and Ben Het's assistant medic occupied the mountaintop with one hundred Montagnard strikers. When they came under attack, Commo Willy just happened to be on the radio that had to relay their messages for them to Kontum, B-24 headquarters. Camps throughout that area of the highlands listened with respect for a fellow SFer as the assistant medic transmitted and adjusted artillery fire with his lower jaw shot off from an AK-47 round.

It was later learned that some of the NVA refused to attack the mountaintop a second time, because the SF-trained Yards fought so fiercely. The NVA commander reportedly pulled out a US Army .45 automatic and shot one of the soldiers between the eyes at point-blank range.

The NVA charged out of the night jungle once more and overran the FSB. Lieutenant Leopold was shot through both thighs and captured along with six of the Montagnard strikers. The six Yard strikers stated that Leopold was initially bandaged, and they were all taken to an old French fort in Laos. The Yards said that Leopold was placed inside a barbed wire cage and was last seen being carried north up the Ho Chi Minh Trail. They escaped the third day and made it back to Ben Het. They also reported that Soviet tanks continued to roll into and out of the fort the whole time they were prisoners.

The Kontum Mike Force choppered in the day following the attack and found the assistant medic, whose name I didn't know, dead. Jaw shot away, he had NVA soldiers lying all over the mountaintop in front of him. He was in a sitting position, propped against a tree, M-16 in his hands. Three dead Montagnards lay across his legs, apparently having died trying to protect him.

All the men in the A-camps who heard about his death probably thought to themselves, *That's how I want to go if I have to go; he was SF all the way.*

The memory of the sound of the brave gravely wounded NCO adjusting fire and giving spot reports with no lower jaw haunted the All-American-looking Sergeant Williams from then on. The image of the fellow lieutenant, bandages around each thigh, being carried in a barbed-wire cage on the shoulders of khaki-clad NVA soldiers still haunts me. As a matter of fact, Lieutenant Leopold was another MIA whose capture would haunt all SFers from that time on.

In the case of the capture of Lieutenant Leopold, near Ben Het, the NVA soldiers weren't as brave as they had been in some of the pitched battles along the border, but the officers surely knew how to motivate their men.

Coincidentally, nobody else occupied that fire support base where the two Ben Het men were overrun until several months later, when the assistant medic from Dak Pek and I with one hundred strikers from Dak Pek occupied the very same positions.

The mountain where the FSB was located was a Mae West mountaintop due east of the camp of Ben Het. The south end of the FSB was occupied by a Fourth Infantry Division artillery battery with a company of infantry providing a defensive perimeter around it. The north peak of the mountain held the Dak Pek unit and a saddle ran between the two peaks. Like most FSBs, the jungle had been defoliated off the cap of the mountain; foxholes, trenches, and bunkers had been dug in and contructed. Outside the line of trenches was a perimeter lined with triple-strand concertina wire, trip flares, and noisemakers.

When I arrived, I immediately sent the Yards out to revise the perimeter security. The Jeh strikers had learned the hard way that most American units were predictable in the way they set up their perimeters. Triple-strand concertina was viewed by some American commanders as an effective barrier, when in reality NVA sappers, in training in North Vietnam, had contests to see who could slip through it the fastest. Most sappers could pass through triple-strand concertina as if it were a simple hedgerow. Noisemakers and trip flares were set up about shin height with trip wires that hung loosely from tree to tree or bush to bush. But the NVA point men walked with no trousers on so they could feel trip wires with their bare shins.

I had the strikers move the trip wires for the trip flares and booby traps. They also loosened the pins on everything. Then they unscrewed the tops off the HE hand grenades and screwed smoke grenade tops into them. Next they wired the grenades to trees along the edge of the jungle. Trip wires were attached to the rings on the grenades and one side of each of the pins was bent and broken off, so the wire could pull it out more easily. With the smoke grenade fuses in them, the grenades would go off a second after the pin was pulled instead of four to six seconds like the normal fuses. When the strikers moved the trip wires and added those of the grenade booby traps, they made the wires very tight and at waist level. This made them harder to detect and easier to spring. It also got them up off the ground so barking deer and other small animals wouldn't spring them.

Next Nhual and I picked out small patches of undergrowth where NVA might try to hide if sneaking up to the perimeter or dive into if fired upon. I had the Yards place razor-sharp bamboo punji stakes in the ground under the bushes, so anyone diving into them or hiding in them would be impaled on the stakes. I then had the CIDG lay tight, ankle-high tanglefoot barbed wire zigzagging in every direction underneath the triple-strand concertina wire. Punji stakes were also wired onto the concertina, pointing inward, so infiltrators would, at the very least, get cuts and scratches.

The medic and I sat in front of a small fire the first evening, drinking hot coffee and telling war stories. I couldn't help thinking about the fact that just a few short months before, the lieutenant who went through the POW camp with me was wounded, taken prisoner, and hauled off to North Vietnam. The assistant medic on his team had been killed at the same time, and it all had happened on the very spot where we were now sitting. Full darkness fell, and we turned in for the evening.

Dai-uy Tran Van Linh was born in 1942 in Hanoi, North Vietnam. He was an infantry company commander with the 24th NVA Regiment and was assigned to over-run the new CIDG unit on the north end of the mountain where the 24th had the great victory a few months earlier.

Earlier in the year, he participated in the assault on Ban Me Thuot during the Tet Offensive. During that siege, he was a lieutenant and platoon leader and was involved in the overrunning of FULRO headquarters at Buon Ale-A. Numerous Montagnards were captured, then lined up and mowed down by a firing squad. That included men, women, and children, after the women were all gang-raped by the NVA soldiers. Some of the FULRO's top cadre and best fighters were killed that day. Sixteen FULRO people were captured and taken prisoner.

Linh wasn't a really strong leader, but he just happened to be there, so he was promoted personally by the commanding general. It probably didn't hurt that the officer's younger sister, a real knockout, gave the general super blow jobs on a regular basis when he was out in the field, where his favorite mistress couldn't find out about her.

Overrunning the SF-led Montagnards at Ben Het would be his first real test of command. Deep down he knew he didn't have the command skills and toughness of the officer who led the attack and capture of Lieutenant Leopold, but he would have to do his best. He must not "lose face." That was a fate worse than death for the Vietnamese, and in his case, his battalion commander might just blow his brains out, even if his sister was sucking off the CG.

Captain Linh, hiding in a deep valley due north of Ben Het, walked around his headquarters bunker holding hands with his first sergeant. They weren't gay—it was Vietnamese custom, and the two men were deep in conversation. The early evening patrols had returned with sketches drawn of my perimeter, indicating listening posts, machine gun emplacements, and the command post, where I would be staying.

I took a swallow of coffee, offered a Lucky to the medic, and lighted both cigarettes. I stared at the ground, deep in thought.

"What's up, Lieutenant Eastwood, stoned?" the medic asked.

Clint Eastwood had become my nickname, jokingly given to me by Harry Boyle before his death. I didn't really mind, as Eastwood was my hero in those days, and I took the joke as a compliment. Being a Green Beret officer in those days, just a couple of years after having been a pimple-studded high school loser, I fantasized trying to live up to an unrealistic Hollywood-type image.

I snapped back to reality and said, "No, I was just thinking about a buddy of mine—several, actually."

"Who?" the *Bac-si* asked.

I replied, "Big son of a bitch, one of the nicest guys you'd ever want to know. His name's Dick Wright, a first lieutenant also. He was one of the lieutenants I went through training with in the Seventh Group at Fort Bragg. Dick's a full-blooded Cherokee Indian, so everyone calls him 'Cherokee.' "

"What made you think about him?"

"Oh," I said, "I ran into him when I was in Nha Trang meeting with the old man. You know the little mountains that you can see just outside Nha Trang?"

"Sure, I remember them," the medic said.

"I went into the Group commo center to check on the latest news around country, and the call came in that a company from the Nha Trang Mike Force was in heavy contact up on one of the mountains. I found out that Cherokee Wright was in charge and the spot report came in that an American was one of the wounded."

"Was it him?"

I continued, "I bummed a jeep and took off for the hospital and arrived the same time the first medevac came in. A number of Yards were taken off and, sure enough, Dick Wright hopped off, saw me, and gave me a big grin."

The medic asked, "He wasn't wounded?"

"He was dirty," I said, "but other than that, he looked fine. Cherokee made sure his Yards were all tended to, then he walked over to me grinning like he had been at a party. I said, 'Hey, Cherokee, how's it going today?' And he said, 'Aw, not too bad, except some Commie son of a bitch shot my thumb off.' Then he held his hand up and his thumb had been shot off cleanly right at the edge of his hand."

"Sir, you're shitting me," the medic said, "I mean about him laughing and grinning. You mean he wasn't in shock or screaming in pain by then?"

"That's nothing," I said. "Cherokee walked along next to me from the helipad, acting like just another friendly guy shooting the shit. He wouldn't let any medics touch him. In the hospital there was a waiting room, and he sat down in a chair and bummed a cigarette from me and sat there asking questions about guys who were at Bragg with us."

"I'll be fucked!"

I continued, "Two doctors talked to a medic and ran over to Cherokee. They grabbed his arm and looked at his missing thumb and about shit themselves. Both of them tried to get him to go into the treatment room, but he yanked away. Now Dick Wright is one of those big, bad, stronger than hell, quiet types, and if he doesn't want to be moved, nobody's going to move him. He smiled and spoke softly, like he always did, and said, 'Sorry, Doc, but I'm talking to my friend here, and I'm going to keep talking to him, until you or somebody comes and assures me that every one of my men who got wounded is in surgery or being stitched up and are totally cared for. Okay?' "

"Your friend is definitely SF, sir," the medic said.

"Yes, he damned sure is," I answered. "The doctor's face just kind of turned several shades of colors, and he told Dick that he would check on all his men and make sure that they were being well taken care of. Dick just smiled and calmly said, 'Fine, Doc. You do that, then you can come and put a bandage on my hand, or whatever you guys have to do.' "

"I'll be fucked," the medic repeated.

"So was Lieutenant Wright," I said, "But you couldn't tell it by his smile."

We both shook our heads and I stared at the ground again. There were hot coals in the fire we sat by and hardly any illumination came from them, but plenty of warmth. I was careful not to stare into the coals, as it could cause night blindness for several precious minutes if we got hit by NVA. Like the Native American of old, I felt the fire's warmth, but I looked at the ground next to the fire or at a point beyond it, but never right at it. If I had to feed sticks or wood into it, I closed one eye. That was for a very simple reason. If your eyes are accustomed to the darkness and you suddenly look at light, you become night-blind for several minutes, but if you keep one eye closed, when you look away into the darkness again the eye that was open will adjust within a second or two.

The medic said, "Lieutenant, you're staring again. You said several buddies?"

I took a drag on my Lucky Strike and blew smoke rings toward the coals.

"No breeze tonight," I said. "Remember the lieutenant I became friends with that was with CCN out of Da

Nang? He came in with a team and launched out of our camp several weeks ago, dark hair, real funny, remember him?"

The *Bac-si* replied, "Yeah, stayed in your bunker. You both got pretty fucked up on rice wine. Of course, when don't you do that, Lieutenant?"

I knew the medic was joking, but nevertheless I felt my ears burning as I got angry then quickly cooled myself down.

I said, "You know Marble Mountain, just outside Da Nang?"

"No, sir, never been to Da Nang."

"I haven't either, but right before we came here, I got word, he got into shit with NVA on Marble Mountain and his position got overrun. Everybody *di di maued,* only he got chased into some caves by a shitload of NVA. He came out of a cave on a ledge where several people saw what was happening through binoculars. He was completely surrounded by NVA soldiers and was down with two leg wounds and this NVA officer walked up to him, cocked a pistol, and pointed it at his face."

I paused and looked down again, taking another drag on my cigarette.

"So what happened?" the sergeant asked.

I went on, "Talk about being SF. He knew the NVA was going to shoot him, so they said it looked like he spit at him, but he definitely gave the officer the finger and laughed in his face before the little yellow fucker pulled the trigger."

"Son of a bitch, Lieutenant. Remind me not to be a friend of yours. Any more buddies get killed lately?" the medic said sarcastically.

I looked up and sighed, then cleared my throat.

The medic was embarassed, "Sorry, sir, I didn't figure there was."

"Another buddy that went through training with me in the Seventh Group just went under. He went down SF, too," I said. "He was with a camp east of here. He was ordered to overrun a hilltop loaded with NVA in concrete-reinforced bunkers. His Yards got chopped up and were pretty scared about a second try, but that was his mission. He got them on line, got out in front of them, and charged up the hill. They overran the NVA and took the position, but he took three sucking chest wounds. He patched himself up—with help from his NCO, he covered the wounds with plastic wrappers from field bandages."

The medic interrupted: "To make an airtight seal."

I nodded. "He was so weak when the dust-off came, he couldn't fucking stand up, hardly, but he said he wouldn't get on the chopper, because there was just enough room for all his wounded Yards. When they came back with a second chopper for him, he'd already bought it."

"We going to get killed here, Lieutenant?" the NCO asked.

"No, we're SF, Sergeant," I answered, staring into the other young man's eyes. "We never lose. Even when we do get killed, we win, anyway."

The buck sergeant started to smile, a little at first, and then he broke into a broad grin.

I said, "Hey, you shouldn't be SF if you can't take a fucking joke, right?"

The sergeant washed his cup with coffee and tossed the rest out while he laughed heartily. He stood.

"Right. Going to bed. Good night, sir."

"Night, *Bac-si,*" I said and headed for my log-reinforced muddy bunker.

The squad leader led *Dai-uy* Linh from the east side of the mountain around the north end and to the west. Everyone was in place to make the probes.

Dai-uy Linh made one mistake when he sent his early patrols out, though. They carefully sneaked in close and drew sketches of my machine gun emplacements, listening posts, and my command post earlier, but they missed one important thing. Like most SF troopers on an operation, I always changed my LPs and automatic weapons positions after it became dark. The CP was still in the same spot, right in the middle and at the top of the hill, but it was empty. I moved into a less conspicuous bunker on the military crest of the hill.

The NVA sapper lead men crept forward on both sides of the perimeter. The squad leader of each held copies of the sketches brought back to *Dai-uy* Linh by the preliminary recon patrols. The sketches not only showed locations of listening posts, the CP, and the machine guns, but locations of trip flares and Claymores as well.

I jumped out of a deep sleep when I heard the loud explosion at the west end of the perimeter. I ran outside my bunker and was greeted by a grinning Nhual. I started grinning, too, when I looked where Nhual pointed.

"It worked," Nhual said enthusiastically.

"Obviously," I said with a broad grin.

The interpreter and I knew what had happened: The point man for the NVA to the west crawled up to what he thought, based on the sketch, was an LP. He found the commo wire going from the little bunker and quietly followed it with his hands to the Claymore mine. All he had to do was turn the Claymore around and get the Imperialists to blow the mine and kill themselves. He carefully grabbed the antipersonnel mine in both hands, lifted it up, and turned it around. The NVA didn't, however, see the little piece of trip wire connected to the leg of the bipod under the mine, nor did he see it pull the ring out of the high-explosive hand grenade buried just under the surface of the dirt.

Several people ran up to Nhual and Mr. Lon, the Cambodian who was the company commander with the CIDG, to find out what happened. The medic and Nhual went to the trenches on one side of the perimeter and warned everyone to stay awake and alert, and I went to the other side and did the same.

I stayed on that side of the perimeter and waited. An hour passed without event, then suddenly two trip flares went off on the east side of the perimeter. A squad of Dega opened up with carbines, while I crouched down and ran across the top of the hill.

Several flashes appeared out of the blackness of the jungle and I heard the sound I hated more than anything else. It was an unmistakable sound that I had heard too many times before—a loud crack, like a whip cracking right over the head or by the ear, followed immediately by a softer whump. Those are the sounds heard when a gun is fired directly at you and the bullets just miss. The crack is the bullet breaking the sound barrier as it passes by and the whump is the muzzle noise from directly in front.

I didn't take time to analyze all of that. I didn't have time. The flashes were immediately followed by the cracks, which were immediately followed by the whump sounds. All of this occurred in less than a half a second, and it took less than the balance of the first second before I was stretched out in a long racing dive downhill toward the trench. I hit the ground in a somersault and rolled while bullets kicked up dirt all around me. I felt my body drop into darkness and crashed into the bottom of the trench.

I immediately popped up with my CAR-15 on automatic and sprayed the jungle, where I saw flashes. A tracer spewed out of my rifle and was followed by three tracers in a row with the second burst. I already had a new magazine in my hand and ejected the old one, popped it down the front of my shirt, and slammed home the new magazine. I fired again.

Like many SFers, I loaded all of my magazines with eighteen rounds instead of the full twenty, because the M-16 magazines, in those days, had very weak springs. I always made the thirteenth round a tracer, so I knew I was near the end of the magazine, and then the last three rounds were tracers to signal the empty magazine. I ejected and threw an empty magazine down the open neck of my shirt, and retrieved a new one from one of the pouches of the BAR ammo belt I wore. I carried three loaded magazines, upside down to keep out dirt, in each pouch, with a fourth magazine lying sideways across the other three.

Another trip flare popped a little to my left front and another section of the perimeter opened up. I ran to that section followed closely by Nhual. The Dega were opening up, several with M-2 carbines fired on full auto.

I jumped out of the debris-filled trench and shouted, *"Dei-ei bang! Dei-ei bang!"*

I yelled at the Yards not to shoot and Nhual repeated his cries. When the two got together, the medic caught up.

I said to the interpreter and the NCO, "They are crawling in and setting off our trip flares, so we will fire our weapons, and they can pinpoint our positions. They want to update their reports on where we are located. *Bac-si*, take four men and get more HE grenades from the ammo bunker and pass them out. Tell the Yards to use grenades—they can't pinpoint where they're coming from. Ba Nua, tell the men not to shoot unless they see a definite target: M-79s and hand grenades only."

Nhual and the medic took off without even responding. It was a time for doing, not a time for talking.

Two trip flares went off on the north end of the perimeter and I took off in that direction. Montagnards started firing back and suddenly one of my two M-60 machine guns opened up from the bunker on the northwest corner of the trench. I tried to shout above the chatter and explosions going off all around. There was no way I could be heard. Several bullets sent dirt onto my shins, and it suddenly dawned on me that I was exposed.

I ran to the machine gun bunker and dived through the doorway of the log-roofed mud bunker. The Montagnard was so busy firing at the jungle, he didn't even know I was there. I grabbed the short, stocky Montagnard by the neck and the seat of his pants and flung him backward through the bunker door. The Montagnard lay on his back looking up at me with pain, anger, and then fear in his eyes. The strikers' fire slowed dramatically. Nhual ran into the bunker.

I was furious, as Nhual looked from the striker on his back to me and back again.

I shouted, *"Ba Nua,* tell him nobody ever taught him to fire his machine gun at night!"

Nhual translated and I continued, "Tell him the only time, ever, he fires it at night is if we are being overrun!"

Nhual translated and the man spoke quickly.

Nhual said to me, *"Trung-uy,* he is a good man and is very ashamed of himself. He will never fuck up with the M-60 again."

"Okay," I said.

I reached down and gave the Montagnard a hand up. We grinned at each other and I pulled a cigarillo out of my pocket and stuck it in the Yard's lips, then whipped out my lighter and lit the man's cigar as well as my own.

I grabbed a hand grenade off his harness, pulled the pin, and stuck it in the little man's hand. The Jeh warrior's eyes bulged about five times their normal size, and he threw the grenade toward the NVA as far as he could. He stood on the edge of the trench, frozen from shock, while Nhual and I ducked. My hand shot out and grabbed the little man, yanking him down. The grenade exploded, and we heard a scream.

I grinned at the striker while Nhual laughed. I patted the man on the back and handed him another cigar. Nhual and I took off down the trenchline, warning those who still had not been told not to shoot.

The west side of the perimeter suddenly lit up and a

grenade booby trap went off with a loud explosion at the same time. This time one of the sappers got tangled up in the wire and made a sitting duck for the CIDG who poured it on him. Miraculously, he received one grazing wound but tore his skin in several places on punji stakes and the wire as he headed for the shadows as if his ass had caught fire.

Several strikers started to fire back at the NVA and I shouted, *"Dei-ei! Dei-ei bang! My dei-ei tiem gal-nat!"*

Suddenly a loud voice came from the jungle shadows in fairly good English, "Fuck you, American!"

I just got mad. I grabbed three grenades from Nhual and shoved them into the cargo pockets of my tiger suit. I didn't know why, but I got pissed as I hadn't in a long time. Nhual clutched at my arm as I jumped out of the trench and ran toward the barbed wire firing my CAR-15 on full auto.

At the barbed wire trip flares illuminated the whole eerie scene, and I pulled the pin on a grenade and held it behind my back.

I faced the darkness of the giant trees in front of me and yelled, "Fuck you and Ho Chi Minh, you Communist piece of shit! Shoot me! Shoot me! You fucking pussy, I fucked your mother and sister last night! Ho Chi Minh eats pig shit!"

A voice finally yelled, "Fuck you!"

I threw the grenade right at the voice. I pulled the other two grenades out, yanked the pins, and threw both as fast as I could, one to the right of the first one and the other to the left. With the second grenade, there was a scream and some moans. I turned and climbed back up to the line of foxholes.

The medic stood next to Nhual and grinned at me as he dropped into the bunker, his sides heaving with exertion and acute adrenaline flow.

The medic finally said, "With all due respect, Lieutenant, I heard you were fucking crazy in deep shit. You really are!"

I looked up at him, shoved a cigarillo in my mouth, lighted it with my best Clint Eastwood imitation, and blew out a puff of smoke.

Then I stood up and said softly, "The Commie gook shouldn't have yelled at me, if he can't take a fucking joke."

Then for dramatic effect, I brushed past the sergeant, walked on, and checked on other strikers down the trench line. I could feel the NCO's eyes staring at my back.

Everything got quiet. The medic and I both went back to bed, after a while, but both of us slept with our boots on, guns at hand, as always. Away from everyone's sight, I shook so badly I could hardly light my cigarette as I sat up on the dirt bed and tried to keep from vomiting.

"Yeah, Clint Eastwood," I whispered to myself in the darkness.

The gastrointestinal cramps passed, as did the nausea, and I lay down.

The heavy probe came an hour before dawn, but this time I told Nhual to spread it along the eastern and northern parts of the perimeter for every man to hug the bottom of their bunkers and foxholes. I got on the Prick 25 and called the Fourth Division artillery battery and called for 105 fire. They were too close, so I had them fire the four-deuce mortar and the 81s they had. I walked the fire from the mortars along the edge of the jungle and along the barbed wire. I then got the howitzers to fire along the north part of the perimeter. At some spots the rounds landed fifteen feet from the line of foxholes and bunkers. The NVA got the hell out of Wichita.

At daybreak several patrols were sent out and came back later with reports of numerous blood trails. Mr. Lon himself took the patrol that went down the east side of the mountain. The squad-size patrol ran into an entire company of NVA about 0830 hours and got pinned down. One Cambodian and ten Montagnards with World War II weapons were kind of a tough match for a whole company of well-equipped, hardened NVA. Even so, the Dak Pek strikers held their own.

I got a FAC there quickly from Dak To, and he brought in two F-100 Phantom jets. Mr. Lon had to speak with Nhual over the Prick 25 in Vietnamese. Nhual translated the words to me. I in turn relayed the messages to the FAC, who spoke directly to the jets.

Nhual, the young assistant medic from Dak Pek, and I were treated to a sight that was probably not seen by many infantry people in war. The fire fight was taking place right at the eastern base of the mountain. The mountain was so steep that during a follow-up patrol I literally stepped down from little tree trunk to little tree trunk like on a giant ladder. It actually was almost straight up and down. Therefore, when the jets swept in and made their air strikes, the three of us watched the aircraft from up above instead of from below it or off to the side. As usual the US Air Force came through with flying colors and kicked some tail.

Three days later we returned to Dak Pek, along with all of the strikers. I went on numerous operations all around Dak Pek, at Ben Het, at Dak Seang, near Dak To, west of Polei Kleng in the Plei Trap Valley, and into Cambodia illegally. I never wanted to kiss the ground at Dak Pek, as when we came back from Ben Het. Knowing Leopold and knowing that the Dak Pek assistant medic and I and one hundred Yards were going in where the Ben Het assistant medic went under, Leopold got captured, and they were with one hundred Yards—well, it simply scared the ever-loving shit out of this old-young lieutenant from Dak Pek.

The medic and I headed straight to the shower room. We shaved off two weeks of beard growth. Special Forces believed in traveling light, so most men did not shave while out in the jungle. Many COs of conventional units really had a problem with that if an SF unit was working OPCON for them, but the attitude was as I often said: "They shouldn't work with SF if they can't take a fucking joke." The two of us soaked up the water and took off for our bunkers.

With a towel wrapped around my waist, I took the underground tunnel that ran from Nhual's bunker by the shower room to the doorway of the TOC. I climbed the steps into the four-deuce pit and down the steps to my bunker, turned on the light, and stopped short. Ning lay on my bunk, a beautiful yellow flower tucked into her shiny black hair. Yellow petals spread over her large golden breasts and flat tummy. She smiled broadly.

Ning spoke with a husky voice. "My warrior comes home from jungle. You take gun, shoot enemy. Now, you take gun, shoot me with *beaucoup* love. I love you, number one thou."

I felt like a howitzer.

The following day, Hazel and her Montagnard assistant cooks prepared a great lunch of steaks, salads, baked potatoes, and pie for the A-team. It seemed as if everyone in the camp was "up." As with most Special Forces medics, *Bac-si*, the team medic, had to be called several times on the field phone, because he had so many patients to tend.

When he walked in the door, a young sergeant with an ever-present smile, he just kept saying over and over, "Son of a bitch! Son of a bitch!"

Commo Willy started laughing because of the strange behavior and said, "Hey, *Bac-si*, what the hell are you talking mumbo jumbo about?"

"Oh, never mind," the medic said, sitting down at his place at the long table. "Son of a bitch!"

I started laughing also and Commo Willy made a circle over his temple with his finger while crossing his eyes. Both of us laughed at the secret joke.

I said, *"Bac-si,* have you been out in the sun all day?"

"Huh!" the medic said as if coming out of a trance. "Oh, no, no, sir. I'll show you what happened after lunch."

"Okay," I said as I bit down into my New York strip, thanks to some Air Force supply sergeant who just loved getting captured AK-47s and other war souvenirs.

Commo Willy and I looked at each other covertly and started quietly chuckling again, but we both lost it as we heard the phrase "Son of a bitch!" again.

After the meal I went out in the driveway and cranked up one of the team's two windowless, doorless, topless jeeps. The medic hopped in and I drove him down the driveway past the parade field and the LLDB rattan team house on the right, and the barbershop, school, and storehouse on the left. I turned the jeep left into the driveway right before the front gate and pulled up in front of the long white building with the red cross painted on the roof. The medic and I pointed and laughed at the now-familiar spitting cobra that regularly sunned itself around the steel capital *H* that marked the camp's helipad in front of the dispensary.

We walked into the building and I nodded to the smiling Montagnard assistant helpers.

"What the hell happened, Doc?" I asked, still puzzled.

"I'll show you, sir," the medic said and led the way into the dispensary office.

He pulled out a big ledger and handed it to me.

"You know that I have everyone sign in or make an *X* when they come here for sick call every morning?" he said.

"Yeah," I replied, opening the ledger. "What about it?"

I turned to see Commo Willy looking over my right shoulder.

The medic said, "Turn to today's log and read the signatures."

I turned the pages until I reached the one for that day. I moved my finger down the long list of names and occasional X's as I read them off and Commo Willy read over my shoulder. My finger stopped on a signature that read: VIET CONG.

"Son of a bitch!" Commo Willy and I shouted at the same time.

5

Sabotage

COMMO WILLY LOOKED DOWN at his hand and saw two pairs, queens and fours.

"Cards," Joe Howard declared, a cigarette hanging out of the corner of his mouth and the deck in his left hand.

He squinted as the smoke curled up and passed across from the end of the cigarette. Commo Willy tossed his three of clubs down on the felt-topped stone poker table in the American team house. Joe Howard smiled, slid one card off the top of the deck, and spun it in front of Commo Willy. Don Williams licked his lips and reached for the card. A bourbon and Coke was set down in front of his hand, and he looked up at Lee, the Vietnamese barmaid who served drinks in the Dak Pek team house. Don smiled and picked up the card, put it with the other four, and slowly peeled it back. Queen of hearts, he had drawn to a full house.

"You opened," Joe said.

Commo Willy turned his eyes toward John T. Williams, the new assistant commo man, and said, "Ole *Bacsi,* raised. I'll check to the power."

Don't tip your hand, Commo Willy thought. *He raised, he'll bet high, then bump him.*

Two figures walked through the darkness across the American hill. I wore a towel around my waist and a quick-draw western holster with a .357 magnum above the towel. Ning wore only her black *atok* and a beautiful smile. We held hands as we walked slowly and looked up at the stars.

Six shadows stood back behind us, looking in every direction—the ever-present bodyguards assigned by the FULRO to watch over me. Needless to say, the Vietnamese and I didn't get along very well. I did, at that time, however, plan to spend the rest of my life with the Montagnards.

On the southern side of the crest of the American hill, there was a line of doorways. First there was an ammunition bunker, and then west of it was a door going into a bunker containing the generator that ran the electricity for the camp. Above them, along the driveway, was a 60 mm mortar pit.

After that, there was the arms room, where weapons were repaired and a trained Montagnard cut M-2 carbine stocks and gave them pistol-grip handles. These were traded, along with captured NVA weapons, to Air Force pilots and supply people for planeloads of food, booze, and other necessities, such as the dehumidifier found in each American's bunker, the stereo system in the team house, the M-60 main battle tank the team owned but still had not figured out how to transport to the faraway outpost, and other unauthorized goodies.

Past the arms room was the shower room, which had several showers and four sinks and mirrors. A big holding tank in the driveway above the showers held water trucked up each morning from the Dak Poko River.

Just past the showers was the door to Nhual's bunker, where he and his wife and two children lived; and just beyond him were the bunkers of Oh, Tuan, and the other cooks and interpreters.

We walked into the shower room and Ning set our toilet kit on the sink. We both brushed our teeth, then came together and kissed. Ning and I walked over to the showers, turned one of them on, tested the water, and then she took off her *atok* while I removed my towel. We didn't see the pair of slanted eyes that stared at us through the crack near the ceiling, near the arms room door. We slowly and softly washed each other's body.

Before my bodyguards moved down near the doorway, a shadow walked along the row of doorways and slipped into the ammunition bunker. Another shadow squatted down outside the bunker door, an M-16 carbine in his hand, and acted as a lookout for the other. The Vietnamese man inside held a small flashlight in his mouth.

Earlier, in the safety of his own bunker, he had shed his ARVN army uniform with the prestigious LLDB patch on it and opted for less conspicuous black pajamas. His hands expertly twisted the nose cap on a 60 mm mortar HE round. He removed the fuse and replaced it with one adapted from a smoke grenade. The correct fuse he held between his knees, while he carefully inserted the booby-trapped fuse.

"Psst!" came the sound from his partner.

He didn't move. He didn't breathe.

"Choi oi!," the saboteur whispered to himself in the darkness, *"Choi doc oi!"*

Sweat ran down his cheeks and dropped onto his black pajamas. He wondered why he hadn't worn his army uniform. If discovered, and in his LLDB uniform, he could just act arrogant, as if he owned the place. He didn't care if the Americans were suspicious of him, just as long as they couldn't prove he was a spy.

He was an LLDB sergeant, even if his stripes were supposedly purchased for him in Pleiku by his father. Actually, his father had been killed by the French at Dien Bien Phu, and the impostor-father was really his commanding officer, a full colonel in the North Vietnamese Army. The spy, a captain in a military intelligence unit, was assigned to pose as a South Vietnamese army sergeant with the prestigious Special Forces, the *Luc Luong Dac Biet.*

The sabotage of the 60 mm mortar round was a simple tactic that was part of the "softening" process. Chairman Mao and Uncle Ho both taught that revolution and guerrilla warfare could not flourish where people were happy with their leadership. The sabotage of the mortar round might cause a mishap, but it could also make the Americans more cautious when they used their weapons.

The NVA didn't really come up with the idea themselves. American Special Forces troopers, in several top secret units, and wearing uniforms and carrying equipment that were completely "sterile," had for several years been infiltrating into NVA staging areas and division headquarters areas in North Vietnam and Laos for direct action missions. One of the most common of these was to take apart 7.62 mm bullets, used in SKSs, AK-47s, and RPG machine guns. The SF men simply poured out the gunpowder and replaced it with composition C-4 plastic explosive and put the bullet back together. The team then exfiltrated and let the chips fall where they might. Later the hapless soldier ending up with that bullet would, at some point, take aim at a target, fire his weapon, and end up having the bolt go through his eye and skull, or blow part of his head off. It made NVA in the man's unit a little less careful about the way they aimed their weapons.

The LLDB sergeant knew that he could bluff his way out of trouble with *Dai-uy* Hoe, the camp commander, if he got caught in the American's ammo bunker. First of all, half of the LLDB team were Communist infiltrators, so they would back him up. Hoe cared only about looking good and making money, but not necessarily in that order. He had a very lucrative black market going at Dak Pek and totally controlled the aircraft passes for the hapless Montagnards wanting to travel to Kontum or Pleiku. Stuck at Dak Pek, the highly paid mercenaries had two choices: They could spend their money on exorbitantly priced goods supplied by *Dai-uy* Hoe, or they could use their money to start cooking fires. The spy knew that Hoe didn't want to kill his "golden goose," so he could be controlled.

The Americans could just become targets of LLDB harassment, if they raised too much stink. Trying to make the Americans lose face was almost a hobby with the Vietnamese counterparts anyway, so he might be able to wiggle out of trouble, if caught.

He saw his partner ease back into the shadow of the doorway, so he didn't even breathe. The man in the door watched a stocky bodyguard come around the edge of the shower room and stand underneath the spot where they were looking through the crack. The two men waited, and after five minutes, they heard a man and a woman leave the shower room, laughing and talking. One second the bodyguard was there; a second later, he was simply gone.

The two Vietnamese breathed a sigh of relief and got the hell out of Dodge.

Three days later most of the team assembled for the latest pastime, firing weapons. For several weeks the team members finished work, had supper, and assembled around one of the many weapons on the American hill. We would BS and take turns firing weapons, sometimes challenging one another in various contests. One night we even sent a jeep down to the next village north of the camp, Dak Jel Luk, and gave the village chief two fifty-pound bags of rice in exchange for the one bag we took turns firing M-79 grenades at. One of the guys finally scored a direct hit and blew the bag to hell and back. The villagers enjoyed the show, so they didn't even complain about the tripod and little rice hootch that was blown up with the bag.

Another early evening one guy went down to the Dak Poko carrying an HT-1 radio. He threw items one by one into the fast-moving current and the team members took turns firing at them with the easternmost .50 caliber machine gun. When an item finally sank, the guy at the river threw new things in.

One of the favorite pastimes was to set a four-hole rocket launcher on several sandbags. Somehow the team had acquired thousands of 2.75 rockets, which were ideal to expend on just screwing around. The rocket launcher was aimed due west and the end was tilted into the air. Commo Willy set up a 12-volt jeep battery and provided some commo wire with the ends stripped. The positive and negative wires were attached to the respective positive posts on the rocket tail and the tail fin. The other ends of the wires were then touched to the posts on the automotive battery, and the rockets would take off toward the nearby border into Laos, hopefully landing somewhere in the midst of the Second NVA Division and other units moving rapidly up and down the Ho Chi Minh Trail.

Several weeks after the saboteurs made their way into the American bunker, I was summoned to Nha Trang, Fifth Special Forces Group headquarters, for a secret meeting with the group commander, Colonel Aaron. At the meeting, sergeants from two other A-camps in the Central Highlands and I were warned that intelligence reports indicated that the three of us might be a high-ranking cadre in the FULRO resistance movement. We three were given a lecture about the government of South Vietnam being the ally of the United States. The FULRO wanted to overthrow the government in Saigon and take back the Central Highlands for the Montagnards. We were warned that we were each facing thirty years in Fort Leavenworth if we were indeed involved in the FULRO and were caught, tried, and convicted.

At the camp, several days after I left, some of the team members decided to fire the 81 mm and the 60 mm mortars. A number of rounds were carried out of the bunker and placed next to the pit. Larry Crotsley took over as the man who fired the rounds from the 60 mm and the team heavy-weapons sergeant, a solid SF E-7, Tom Weeks, fired the 81 mm. Various targets were picked outside the camp perimeter.

Seated on the sandbags bordering the 81 mm pit but facing Crotsley on the 60 mm was Commo Willy's boss, the chief radio operator for the team, Sergeant First Class Harry Boyle. Redheaded and always smiling, he was very popular with the team members and the Montagnards. Harry drove everyone crazy—he was always showing them photographs of his beautiful Latin wife. Living in southern California and unable to speak a word of English, she was en route to Hawaii to meet Harry there for R and R. He was to leave the next day. Harry had spent plenty of time in South America when he was assigned to the Eighth Group in Panama. That's where he met his bride.

Harry was famous for showing her picture and saying, "Have I ever showed you a picture of my wife? Look at her. Isn't she beautiful?"

The team member, seeing the photo for the umpteenth time would usually say, "Yeah, Harry, she's gorgeous."

It had become almost a joke among the team members, but it also touched the hearts of these macho men deep down beneath the masks of invincibility. Harry Boyle was certainly in love with his wife. SFers joked that one of the qualifications to wear a beret and flash was to have a divorce. The other qualifications were to have pissed in the Mekong River and to have called Batman a pussy. The fact that Harry carried on so much about his wife got to his teammates down deep.

The one thing, however, that was unnerving to the men was Harry's follow-up to showing the photograph.

He would get very serious and say, "I just can't get

killed, man. I love my wife too much, and she'll be all alone. I just can't get zapped."

Everyone who heard these words always reassured Harry and made light of his comments, but his words also gave them a grim reminder that this indeed was a war, not training.

Harry sipped on a Budweiser while Larry fired the 60 mm at a dead tree due west of the camp where the jungle had been cleared away. Larry was bracketing in his shots by adjusting the elevation and line of the mortar, without using sights. He instead used "Kentucky windage and Tennessee elevation."

Sitting next to Harry was a young E-5 who was a replacement for one of the 403rd ASA NCOs. Sergeant Tomczak was an orphan and a recent high school graduate. He had been in-country less than two weeks and had been assigned to Dak Pek, having arrived earlier that day at 1400 hours, full of piss and vinegar.

The team medic, or *Bac-si*, who was officially known by the Army as Staff Sergeant Aftshower, wore glasses and was around the age of most of the team members, early twenties. A very studious and serious medic, he constantly read the Merck manual and other medical books, trying to increase and improve his medical knowledge. He was liked and respected by the other team members. Usually glued to his work at the dispensary, treating a variety of illnesses and wounds of the thousands of Montagnards in his valley, he decided to take a break. He leaned against the front corner of the team house, watching the firing of the two mortars.

Next to him was a large black Spec-4 from the Fourth Infantry Division at Dak To who had been picking Aftshower's brain all day long. This man, a medic with a conventional Army unit, wanted to learn as much as he could from an SF medic when he had the chance.

SF medics became almost like doctors at the numerous A-camps that dotted the countryside of Vietnam.

While many men burned flags and draft cards and battled the police in the US, decrying the war and the warriors in Vietnam, especially the highly trained Special Forces, Green Beret medics were busy saving the lives of thousands and thousands of Vietnamese, Montagnards, Laotians, Cambodians, Koreans, Americans, and Chinese Nungs in Vietnam. On top of that, they used their off-hours to teach good nutritional habits to the indigenous people.

Behind Aftshower and his eager pupil stood a large master sergeant from MAC-V in Kontum who had been visiting Dak Pek to work with the RuffPuff, the Regional Force/Popular Force village defenders in each of the Yard villages surrounding Dak Pek proper. When the first round left the 81 mm tube, he shot out of the door of the team house, coffee and doughnut in his hand.

The team operations sergeant, Master Sergeant Pickles, was, like Sergeant First Class Tom Weeks, near the end of his tour and getting ready to go back to "the World." At the time, though, he simply wanted to take an "LLDB" and was sitting on the two-holer in the cinder block latrine behind the team house, reading a copy of the in-country-published *Green Berets* magazine. Ironically I, the Civil Affairs/Psy OPs executive officer, and the Admin executive officer of the team were gone, and the team commander was also at higher headquarters. With no officers on-site, Sergeant Pickles was in command.

Commo Willy had been putting in a lot of hours so his boss and buddy, Harry Boyle, could leave on R and R the next day, so he decided to take a hot shower and then hit the hay. He walked across the top of the American hill, wearing flip-flops and his jungle fatigues. Don Williams was tired and ready to recharge his batteries. He opened the shower room door and took one step inside when there was a tremendous explosion. Pieces of shrapnel and debris rained and rattled on the corrugated tin roof of the shower room and Commo Willy flattened himself on the concrete floor.

He heard screams, jumped up, and ran out the door. At the top of the driveway, the first thing he saw was Sergeant Pickles flinging the latrine door open, fatigue pants down around his ankles. He was wiping as fast as possible.

Pickles and Williams looked at each other and simultaneously yelled, "What happened?"

Both men ran toward the front of the team house and saw a giant cloud of smoke obscuring the 81 mm and 60 mm mortar pits. They both thought a big rocket must have come in and destroyed what was left of their A-team who were still at Dak Pek. Working their way through the smoke, they discovered a horrible sight.

When the booby-trapped 60 mm mortar round exploded, it was only a few feet out of the tube, and it sent shrapnel everywhere. Larry Crotsley, who fired the round, was untouched by shrapnel but was blown completely out of the pit and over the side of the hill. He also couldn't hear a thing, but Williams and Pickles, not knowing he was lying stunned just out of sight, figured he was blown into little pieces.

Tom Weeks had just bent over to pick up an 81 mm round and was also protected, by Providence, from shrapnel wounds. He was lying down, however, and was dazed, as he had been knocked over by the body of Harry Boyle, the man who was to leave the next day to see the wife he loved so much. Harry took a large piece of shrapnel through the left eye and left temple and was thrown backward right into Weeks. His body sent Tom across the pit into the wall of sandbags. Harry's feet still lay across the sandbags, and he lay on his back in the bottom of the pit, his good right eye seeming to stare at the blue sky . . . but Harry had been killed instantly.

Next to Harry, the body of the young buck sergeant with the Army Security Agency outfit twitched spasmodi-

cally. He had been hit in the right eye and right temple.
And he, too, had been killed instantly.

Sergeant Weeks stood up, looked around, and shook
his head violently to clear the cobwebs. Something inside
the tough man made him realize what had happened, and
he snapped his brain into action. He checked desperately
for life in the bodies of the two fallen NCOs.

Sergeant Aftshower leaned against the corner of the
team house with blood spurting from both arms. He
grabbed both forearms, trying to cut off the circulation
and slow the bleeding. His left arm, bleeding arterially,
was squirting blood out in a pulsing beat. The E-4 next to
him was untouched but was shaking his head also, trying
to clear the cobwebs. The E-8 behind them went into the
team house, holding his stomach, and collapsed against
the door.

Sergeants Pickles and Williams took in the sight in
sweeping glances and immediately ran to the medic.

White-faced, Aftshower weakly said, "Stop the
bleeding quick! I'm going fast!"

Stripping his belt off, Pickles shouted, "Get the first
aid kit! Fast!"

Commo Willy ran around the corner while Pickles
quickly made a tourniquet around the medic's left arm.
Commo Willy tried to run into the mess hall, but the door
was blocked. He shoved and his hand went right through
the screen, so Williams put his shoulder to it and pushed
forward. The master sergeant from MAC-V lay against
the door frame holding his stomach.

"I'm hit!" he said, face as white as a sheet from
shock.

"Hang on, Sarge!" Tom said, running through and
trying to get the first aid kit as fast as possible.

He ran back, taking it to Pickles, who immediately
started applying pressure bandages on Aftshower.

"Commo Willy, call for medevacs ASAP!" he commanded.

"Wilco, Top," Commo Willy replied and started to take off but stopped briefly. "That E-8 from MAC-v's hit in the gut, Top. He's in the team house."

Pickles said, "We'll get to him in a minute. Hurry!"

Williams took off for the commo room and called for a Medevac helicopter. In the meantime, the Fourth Division medic came to his senses and ran inside to the E-8. He stripped away the man's shirt but couldn't find any wounds. Commo Willy joined him and they both looked but could only find a little blood at the navel.

Pickles came in and checked the man, removing his trousers, but he couldn't find any wounds either. Nevertheless, the sergeant held his stomach and moaned in pain. Pickles and Williams comforted him and treated him for shock. Two weeks later he died of acute intestinal infection in a Pleiku hospital. His wounds apparently had been made by blunt shrapnel not piercing the skin but doing internal damage nevertheless.

Outside, Weeks went from man to man and gave further care to Aftshower.

Larry Crotsley, still dazed, crawled up the hill behind the mortar pit and appeared in the driveway, looking around.

He said, "What happened?"

Weeks said, "Mortar blew up!"

Larry made a face and held his hand up behind his ear cupping it.

He yelled, "What? Can't hear you!"

Pickles and Williams came out the door, carrying the E-8 on a stretcher. The three NCOs talked to Larry Crotsley making sure he was okay, but he couldn't hear anything for several hours.

The dust-off medevac came and Pickles had to force the other sergeants to go on it and get checkups, just to be sure.

The wounded were taken away, while Pickles and Commo Willy watched the medevac fly off into the distance. Both men felt kind of lonely. Ironically, most of the members of Dak Pek's A-team were gone and these two were the only ones left on-site. Two Americans were left alone, deep in the middle of hostile territory: two Americans, about one hundred Vietnamese, and about eight thousand Montagnard tribespeople.

When the medevac helicopter flew out with the wounded and the bodies of the dead, two men watched from a bunker on the Vietnamese hill. Chuckling, they patted each other on the back and toasted each other and Ho Chi Minh with cans of American beer.

The next morning Ning walked to the river, a basket with our dirty laundry on her head. She also carried the laundry of Plar, a cute little seven-year-old orphan girl who had claimed me as her new daddy. Her parents were killed by the Vietcong a few years earlier. The two of us had become attached and I had requested and received application forms to adopt her. She went to Nha Trang with me with promises of presents and fun.

Ning approached the banks of the Dak Poko. The sun played off the ample, firm breasts of the young Montagnard beauty. Her shiny waist-length black hair hung over one of the breasts and blew partially across her face with the morning breeze.

An American GI in a Fourth Division uniform walked out from behind some bushes smiling at Ning. She smiled back, but Ning was troubled by the man's facial gestures and body language. He staggered up to her and stared lustfully at Ning's breasts and rounded hips, barely hidden beneath the black silk skirt.

Thick-tongued, he spoke. "Hey, nice tits, *mamasan.* How about some *bakanook?* We go in bushes and make boom-boom, number one, okay?"

"No," Ning replied, "Go away."

She turned around swiftly. The soldier stepped in front of her, an angry look on his face. He seemed to be drunk and stoned on drugs. Ning was frightened.

"What the fuck's wrong, Co?" he snarled. "Think you're too good for me? Lemme feel those nice tits, huh?"

He stepped forward, hand up. Ning angrily struck it away.

She snapped, "I said, go away! My man come soon! He is *Trung-uy* Bendell, Loo-ten-ant Bendell. He cut you many pieces you touch me! He shoot you! Burn you on fire. He is great warrior and kills many men."

"Yeah, right, baby. Come on, let's fuck?"

The soldier grabbed Ning's wrist, and she spit in his face. He wiped it off, a crazed angry look on his dirty face, and stepped forward, fists balled. Ning covered her face, but he stopped at the sound of guns cocking.

The man and Ning, both surprised, turned their heads, and he found himself staring at the business ends of six M-2 carbines being held by six very tough-looking Montagnards. Ning was amazed. She knew that they could not interfere with an American soldier unless she was about to be killed. But I had not let the ever-present bodyguards go to Nha Trang with me. They were to stay and watch over Ning. Pulling guns on an American soldier was a bold act, but Ning was valuable. They also knew that he was a doped-up deserter who had hidden out and remained behind when his Cloverleaf water purification unit pulled out.

Ning was escorted back up the hill to my bunker, the bodyguards, as usual, keeping a distance away from her on all sides, ready to tackle anything or anyone else wanting to menace the Dega beauty.

A short time later, Sergeants Pickles and Williams were both informed about the Fourth Division deserter.

A half hour after that, the doper saw another Montagnard beauty walking up the hill with laundry. She too was pretty with a great figure, so he followed her to her family's bunker on the Bravo Company's hill. She walked into the underground bunker and handed the laundry to er mother. Her father, an old striker who had also ought with the French, smiled and lit a bamboo pipe.

A chuckle sounded from the doorway and the doper/ drunk GI stood there, a high explosive hand grenade, pin pulled, held up in his hand.

He spoke drunkenly, "I ain't getting no more turn-downs. I wanna fuck her. Come here!"

An hour later Suet, the interpreter, followed by a couple of LLDB ran up the American hill.

Pickles and Williams, eating lunch, heard an LLDB sergeant screaming, "Americans number ten! Americans number ten!"

They walked out of the team house, questioning looks on their faces.

Suet ran up, *"Trung-si* Pickles, Fourth Division GI, *beaucoups* drunk, *beaucoups* drugs. He go Jeh bunker Bravo Company. He drop hand grenade and blow up him, and Montagnard man and wife."

When the two NCOs got to the bunker, the young girl stood outside crying. The sturdy bunker was still in-tact, but inside were the shredded bodies of her mother and father. At the base of the steps of the bunker, Pickles and Williams could find only part of the American's skull, spine, and ribcage. The girl couldn't speak English but knew his intent, so she went to him to save her family. She then took off running, and he was so drunk he dropped the grenade, apparently, and blew them all to kingdom come—at least the husband and wife. The GI was blown to smithereens.

Plar and I arrived by Huey an hour later. I had read about the mortar mishap on the Fifth Group teletype machine. Ning greeted me at my bunker door and threw herself into my arms, sobbing.

Plar watched, puzzled, then walked into the bunker and picked up the puppy, Ambush, that I had bought for her in Nha Trang. She ran out to play with Nhual's son and daughter.

The Vietnamese had been watching her closenes with me, too. One month later the Montagnards foun Plar's raped and beaten body in the barbed wire, anothe victim of the Vietnamese hate of the Montagnards—an me. I buried her with the Jeh at an old graveyard in th jungle, in tribal tradition.

Because of my involvement with the Yards and th feared FULRO, the Vietnamese made a number of assas sination attempts on me over a short period, but God wa watching over me. One of the attempts sent Ning to th hospital and near-death, after drinking poisoned whiske meant for me. Her stomach damaged, she returned t me. Several more of my Montagnard friends, all FULRC cadre, were beaten or stabbed to death during that time

The FULRO leaders weren't the only targets for as sassination or sabotage, though.

In late 1968 Captain Joe Dietrich had been in com mand of Dak Pek for several months. Prior to that, h had commanded the A-team at Plei Me and then th Kontum Mike Force. Joe was respected by, and popula with, the Montagnards as well as the Americans. He an I had recently returned from a long operation in the NV/ stronghold called the Plei Trap Valley, which was farthe south, right at the tri-border of Cambodia, South Viet nam, and Laos.

Every day the weapons NCO checked the head-spac ing and timing on the .50 caliber machine guns. Seve were in camp, and two of them were emplaced in bunker on the American hill. The sergeant would carefully mea sure the timing and headspace with metric gauges, a important detail. If the head-spacing and timing were no properly set, a large .50 caliber shell could rupture in th chamber and kill or maim anyone close to the big gu while it was being fired.

The .50 caliber machine gun was probably the easies weapon to sabotage because of the timing and head-spac ing. The NVA and VC were very aware of this fact.

The American team sold beer they scrounged by trading captured weapons to the Vietnamese, CIDG, and visiting military units. The purchaser just came to the team house and paid a nominal price for the beer and the money went into the team fund.

One evening the LLDB sergeant who booby-trapped the 60 mm mortar round and his helper walked to the American team house. The team was watching a movie, along with cooks, helpers, interpreters, and their families. The two spies bought cans of beer and walked off into the darkness but stopped at the .50 caliber bunker by the American team house.

The LLVC sergeant walked into the sandbagged circle while his helper kept watch. He grabbed the barrel of the .50 caliber with both hands and twisted it in a counterclockwise direction. This twisting of the barrel opened the head-spacing too much, so a shell could explode when the gun was fired.

The next morning the NVA decided to attack the much-picked-on village of Dak Dru Doc once again. The alarm was given and Joe Dietrich shouted out orders to various team members. He personally ran to the .50 caliber above his bunker, near the entrance to the team house. Joe cocked the gun twice and placed his thumbs on the press-down trigger in the rear. I did the same on the .50 caliber machine gun above my own bunker on the west part of the hill. Everyone fired at the North Vietnamese troops outside the village at the north end of the valley. Tracers crossed each other and disappeared into smoke rising up from numerous explosions from the camp's four-deuce and 81 mm mortars, combined with more explosions from recoilless rifle fire.

The battle didn't last too long, with the NVA retreating into the jungle growth north of the village, and they took off for parts unknown.

One of the NCOs yelled, "They're running! They're running!"

Dietrich had disappeared.

Another NCO ran over to me and said, "Hey, Lieutenant, Captain Dietrich's been hit! Right in the crotch!"

I ran toward the edge of the team house, headed toward Dietrich's machine gun. Other team members ran to the commander's position.

I shouted at one, "Call for a medevac quickly and get the medic!"

We pulled up short as Captain Dietrich stood up holding his crotch, which was bleeding profusely. Dietrich, always SF, was laughing heartily.

He cheerfully said, "Someone get the *Bac-si* with a bandage. I've got a hole in me someplace."

His courage in that situation was admired by all the men on the team.

Commo Willy pointed at the blood-soaked groin area of Dietrich's fatigue trousers, laughed, and said, "Oh, Captain Dietrich, is your wife gonna be pissed!"

Joe was, in fact, close to going home. He was medevacked and doctors performed surgery, removing thirty-four pieces of shrapnel from the exploding .50 caliber shell. They had penetrated his penis, testicles, and legs. Dietrich was stitched up, and luckily recovered fully.

The Fifth Group CO came to Joe's hospital ward with a group of people from headquarters. The commander made a big deal out of giving Joe his Purple Heart and pinned it on the sheet over Joe's penis, while an NCO read a hilarious citation that kept mentioning Captain Dietrich's having been wounded in the penis and testicles.

That mishap turned out a little happier than the 60 mm mortar incident, but nonetheless, several pairs of eyes at the Vietnamese hill watched with grim satisfaction as the dust-off carried the wounded team commander away.

Joe Dietrich was replaced by a recently activated reserve captain from Oklahoma, Captain Selders. He was a

nice guy, but I didn't speak with him much. I felt someone new coming into command would have to be there
awhile to find out how the Yards were treated by the
Viets and what was really happening. So much had happened, and I had withdrawn slowly from the Americans
on the team, getting closer and closer to the Dega.

I was also starting to get sick, very sick, and the only
person who knew was Ning. I made her promise not to
tell anyone. I had headaches so severe, I took double and
triple doses of Darvon-65s, which were .50 caliber pain
relievers in regular doses. At night I kept getting fevers
and chills, and I just hoped that it was dengue fever, and
not malaria. I couldn't afford to get ill. A number of
times Ning tried to get the medic for me, but I stopped
her and told her a dust-off would come and take me away
to America.

I was an alcoholic. The product of a broken home, I
had been one of those juvenile delinquents just lucky
enough to have never been caught. I was a class clown
and had no self-esteem at all through junior high and
high school. The Army and Special Forces and OCS, especially, changed all that. The success I had been allowed
to achieve in such a short period of time turned me from
an outgoing but socially awkward young man with no self-
esteem into a still immature but confident young leader. I
had done well in combat. At twenty-one, I had become a
man who would quietly grin to myself, the rest of my life,
whenever I saw wannabee warriors who pick fights at bars
on weekends with other out-of-shape wannabees, or
thump their chests and brag to any who listen what
badasses they are.

More important, I had become the "Tom Jeffords" I
had dreamed about becoming since childhood. As a boy,
all of my dreams were about being the white man taken
in by a proud tribe of warriors, the one white man they
respected and called brother, because he was one of
them, in heart. I now had that, and I didn't want to lose

that. I had a reason for living that was ten times more important than myself.

Shortly after the arrival of Captain Selders an incident happened that could have saved many Montagnards and even some Americans. I quite possibly could have ended up with some medals on my chest that would have made my entire military career for me, and more important to me, the North Vietnamese would have been really pissed. The whole thing also might have delayed the overrunning of Dak Pek, but the entire project was destroyed by military protocol.

I walked down to the Dak Poko one morning with my lover, carrying a bag of bars of soap. While Ning washed some clothes, I went out into the water and started passing out the soap. The Yards lined up on the bank and held their sides laughing while I grabbed wrinkled old ladies and scrubbed their backs and drooping breasts with the soap. I also grabbed little kids and shampooed their hair with the soap. While I was doing this, I gave lectures, with Ning translating, about how soap kills the little demons that live on the skin and crawl into the body.

After half an hour I caught sight of Nhual on the bank with a dirty old woman who was from one of the villages. I walked to the riverbank, knowing Nhual needed to speak to me. I stayed in the water and acted as if I wasn't paying much attention to the stocky interpreter with the intelligent eyes.

"What's up?"

Nhual whispered, "This woman must speak to you, private. Fast."

"Where?" I said.

Nhual answered, "Come to her village, Dak Kiep Nam."

"Can Ning come?" I asked.

"There is much danger," was the grave answer. "You must not bring even the bodyguards."

"I'll be there as soon as I can. Go ahead," I replied.

Nhual and the old lady walked toward the village, a mile distant, the farthest village to the south. Ning watched the whole interchange and I nodded at her to leave.

As I joined Ning on the riverbank, I noticed a Vietnamese watching us from about fifty yards away, near the camp gate. My bodyguards closed around me as I prepared to head back up into the camp, and the head one was within earshot. The Vietnamese was one of the ones that I was sure was another hit man hired to kill me, or he was VC. The man was supposedly a relative of one of the LLDB, but that always seemed to be the convenient generic excuse.

I spoke carefully to the head bodyguard, without looking. "See the *Yuan* watching me?"

The bodyguard said, *"Yuan* man watches *Chung-wi* today, today before, that day before."

I gave Ning a quick kiss on the lips and glanced toward the Vietnamese, still some distance off. The man flushed.

I acted as if I just noticed the man, gave him a broad smile, and whispered through my phony smile, "Slit the bastard's throat."

The bodyguard said, "Number one."

We started up the hill, but I stopped and said to the bodyguard, "I have to be totally alone for a while."

"I know," the bodyguard said and walked away with two others.

The other three stayed with Ning and me. The bodyguards, as usual, hung out, within sight, as we went into the bunker.

Ning said, "Whatchu think?"

I opened my footlocker, pulled out my .357 magnum, removed my jungle fatigue shirt, and tucked the holster into my pants at the small of my back. I grabbed a roll of OD tape, taped the holster against my skin, and replaced my shirt. I pulled a long black-and-silver-handled switch-blade out of the footlocker and taped it below the base of my neck, between my shoulder blades. Then I took a smaller green-handled switchblade with gold inlaid drag-ons in the handle and put it in my left front pocket.

Finally I answered her. "I think I'm getting into some serious shit, honey, but I have no idea what it is."

She helped me into my BAR belt and harness and handed me my CAR-15. I ejected the magazine, checked it, made sure the chamber was empty, flipped the selector to "semi," and pulled the trigger. Next I replaced the magazine and flipped the selector to "safe." I pulled my giant Montagnard knife from its bamboo sheath sewn into the back of the thigh of my trousers, checked the blade for sharpness, and replaced it.

Ning gave me a big hug and said very matter-of-factly, "Do not worry. Even if VC come or something bad maybe, you be top man, no sweat. You do number one thou always same-same."

I looked down into her eyes and gave her a quick kiss.

She grinned broadly and said, "I see you supper."

I winked and said, "Maybe I am supper."

Ning laughed and said, "Maybe me, too, same-same."

We both giggled. I left the bunker, nodded at the bodyguards, and hopped into the quarter-ton parked by the team house. To me it was a jeep, but the Army wanted it to be called a one-quarter-ton truck. I drove off toward another unknown adventure.

I barreled down the hill, zigging and zagging around indigenous, Viets, and Plar's pet dog, Ambush. The black-and-white dog lay in the driveway, lazily shifting his eyes from Vietnamese to Montagnard, knowing in his lit-tle canine brain that each of them wanted to serve him for dinner, but he belonged to the American lieutenant, so they couldn't.

I turned right after going through the sandbagged front gate and headed toward the runway, where C7A Caribous landed several times each week, delivering food and supplies. I went beyond the runway and pulled up short at the steep drop-off to the Dak Pek River, which flowed into the Dak Poko from the mountains out of the west.

A young village girl was carrying a giant stack of firewood on her back, a load most men could not even lift. She walked off the end of a PSP-and-bamboo bridge spanning the narrow but deep river and gave me a big grin. I hopped out of the jeep, crossed the bridge, and started my uphill trek past the villages of Dak Peng Sial Peng and Dak Plei Bom. I arrived at the base of the path going up the hill to Dak Kiep Nam, but a teenage Jeh boy built like a linebacker and caked with mud stepped out from behind some trees.

"Trung-wi, mi chiu ao," the young boy said, asking me to go with him.

I said, *"Ao dei-ei wa chiu. Nhual chiu my ai?"*

The lad said, *"Nhual chiu bri-nal. Trung-wi chiu ao."*

I followed the dirty young man into the jungle. We walked around the base of the village hill and were soon into the thick green foliage. The trail we followed was well worn. I looked down and noticed numerous fresh tracks in the muddy trail. They looked as if they could have been made by Ho Chi Minh sandals. I carefully jacked a round into the chamber of my sawed-off 5.56 mm death dealer and pulled my Jeh knife out. I slipped the blade up under the tape wrapped around my two HE grenades and cut through it. *Thank God for the advice of Charlie Telfair,* I thought.

At a trail intersection I came to the little gnarled woman and Nhual, seated by a fire built right in the middle of the trail.

"This is Charlie country, *Ba Nua,*" I said, "You trying to get us all killed?"

"No, it is safe, Don," Nhual said, calling me by my first name, which he did only in private or when he was sure nobody could understand the informality.

If Nhual told me that it was safe, I knew that it was totally safe, so I relaxed and sat down. Nhual had already made me a canteen cup of coffee, which I drank.

"What's up?" I said between sips.

I lighted a cigar and handed it to the little old lady and lighted another for myself. Nhual didn't smoke.

I felt the pangs of another horrible headache starting. I pulled four Darvon-65s out of my fatigue shirt pocket and swallowed them with water from my canteen. I knew they wouldn't help much, but at least I'd get to float around while the pain was there.

Nhual said, "This lady's son is a sergeant with the local VC. Her son was supposed to meet us here today, but he told her he could only come if he could sneak away without the NVA leader seeing him."

"Why?" I asked.

"You will not believe this," Nhual said, obviously very excited. "You will not believe."

"Try me."

Nhual went on, while the lady watched with fascination, "First of all, she can be trusted."

"Okay," I said.

"Her son is the first sergeant of the two companies of VC. There is really two small companies, because our H-and-I fires killed many," Nhual said. "There is—"

Nhual stopped and turned to the woman, speaking rapidly in Jeh.

He turned back to me and said, "They had many political officers, but now only have eight NVA commanders and political officers with maybe seventy to one hundred Jeh in the two companies. Her son says all Jeh VC fight only because NVA threaten to kill families in villages."

"I know," I said.

"Her son wants to give up to you. He trusts you," Nhual repeated.

"He doesn't know me," I replied. "How can he trust me?"

Nhual told the little old lady something, and they both laughed. I gave him a questioning look.

Nhual went on, "We laugh because all Jeh know you. You are brother to the Jeh. Her son and most of the VC have seen you many times. When you made the country store to kill *Dai-uy* Hoe's black market, all Jeh come to buy dried fish, beads, cloth, many things. Even the VC come, too."

"Son of a bitch," I said, queasy in the stomach and floating several inches above the trail from the Darvon-65s.

Nhual and the woman spoke longer and finally Nhual said, "Her son wants to meet you here in the jungle, no weapons, but only you and me. I will come."

"Unarmed?" I said, "You got to be shitting me, *Ba Nua?*"

"No," Nhual said, "all his men will be unarmed, too."

"All his men?" I almost choked on my coffee. "What do you mean, all his men?"

"I thought you understand. All the Jeh VC want to surrender to you. Her son leads them here. You and I meet them, and we walk into the camp. They know you will not let the *Yuan* shoot them."

"Shit, no, Nhual," I said, "They'll be *Hoi Chanhs.* We'll treat them nice. First, we'll give them food and clothes and get intel from them. Then we'll send them to a *Chieu Hoi* center. They'll be treated good and then can come home. That's how the NVA take vacations. They give up, go to a *Chieu Hoi* center for two weeks, gather intel, rest, and then take off and rejoin their unit."

Nhual went on, "They think NVA are all bullshit. Our H-and-I fires have been making them not sleep long time now. Kill many. Much disease. No food. They say they want you to make they families—ah—their families safe."

"No sweat," I said. "Listen, ask her what the NVA will do when the Yards leave?"

Nhual said, "She told me already. They wait until NVA all sleep, then sneak away sometime."

"No," I said. "Tell them to put guns on NVA and tie them all up. Bring them with them, and we will pay them reward to their families. I will meet them all here tomorrow, right at noon. I won't carry any weapon, but tell them to bring all their weapons and we will pay them a reward for the weapons, too."

"Okay," Nhual said and translated my words to the woman.

Obviously excited, she responded affirmatively.

Nhual said, "She says they will do all you say. Her son will come tonight to get food from her and she will tell him. I will come with you. I believe we will be safe. Hey, you will get Medal of Honor, maybe," he joked.

I said, "Yeah, sure, just like all the other medals guys on A-teams get. All a guy on an A-team *can* get is the Medal of Honor, but only if you get thoroughly zapped. Now I could go to Kontum and work for the B-team and become a fucking hero.

"Come on, let's go home. Tell her, when we come tomorrow, I will bring her a big bag of rice and some beads." Nhual told the old woman and she ran to me and gave me a hug.

I don't remember if I got the chills or not that night; I got so drunk I couldn't remember. That was almost a constant, anyway.

The next day I barely briefed the new team CO and took off with *Ba Nua,* carrying an HT-1 radio. We arrived at the spot an hour early. I chain-smoked cigarettes while we waited, and we discussed which way we would dive, roll, and run if it was indeed a trap. We were there fifteen minutes when I got a call from the CO.

"Peewee Lackey Alpha, This is Peewee Lackey. Over," the voice came over the little black radio.

I said, "Fuck, now what?"

I raised the radio and said, "This is Peewee Lackey Alpha. I cannot talk now. Over."

"Lackey Alpha," the CO said, "you have to come back to camp ASAP. Over."

"What?" I shouted into the radio, "Lackey, do you know what's going on here? I can't come back. Over!"

"Sorry, Alpha," he said to me. "I cannot explain over the radio, but it is not a request, it's an order, and don't develop radio trouble. Over."

I kicked a tree and lifted the radio, "Peewee Lackey Alpha. Out.

I threw the radio on the ground and went into a tirade, kicking trees and punching branches, falling over after one missed kick, I was so angry.

Nhual said, "I will stay."

"Not without me, you won't," I fumed, "I am not taking a bunch of guys out to rescue you if you get captured. Nhual, you do need to explain it all to the woman and tell her we will reschedule with her. That means, make a new time to meet."

I returned to the camp while Nhual went to the village and spoke with the woman. I found the team commander in the TOC with several other team members.

"Captain, can we talk privately?" I said.

We two walked outside and stood in the four-deuce mortar bunker.

I asked, "Captain, do you know how important that was? Do you have any fucking idea, sir? Why did you call me back?"

The CO looked serious. "Sorry, Bendell, I know what you were doing was real important, but we got a three-star general, General William Peers, flying in, and he wants everyone here to give him a briefing."

"A briefing, a fucking briefing," I said in a low voice. I was so angry I couldn't yell.

I went on, "Captain, fuck the Chairborne fucking Ranger! Can't somebody else brief him?"

"No, they can't. You will."

"Yes sir. I'm going to my bunker to change uniforms."

The captain said, "Good idea."

An hour later I was standing in front of the intel maps in the TOC giving my share of the briefing to a general who was blowing smoke in my face from a big thick cigar. Back in "the World," people were thinking about the coming of spring for 1969. On the other side of the globe, however, all I could think about was smashing a big rat dick cigar in a general's face.

That very night I finally fell victim to sabotage, but from Mother Nature. She had a lot more power and savvy than the Vietnamese. I learned then to embrace her as a friend, as she was one enemy who could not be defeated.

For the past month I had lost weight, of course had the severe headaches, and kept getting weaker. By the time it all came to a head, my eyes had turned yellow and my urine was the color of Coca-Cola.

That night my fever went so high I became totally delirious, and Ning, fearing for my life, ran to the medic's bunker and summoned him. I had a fever of 106.4 degrees, and it was climbing. The medic gave me an intravenous injection of quinine and treated me for the fever.

The medic ran to the bunker door, "Lieutenant, you're going home. I'm calling a dust-off and getting a stretcher."

He ran out the door.

Ning looked down into my face, panic on her own. She kissed me all over my face. I smiled weakly and touched her cheek softly. She grabbed my hand and rubbed it against her skin, while she cried her eyes out.

"You must leave Ning forever," she cried.

"But my love will always be with you, Ning," I said.

"Do not die," she commanded, trying to be brave.

"I won't, and if I can't come back, someday I will tell the world about the Montagnard, about what the Vietnamese do to the Dega," I said. "That is even more important than us."

She dropped her head on my chest and cried, softly saying, "I know."

"I love you, Ning, number one thousand," I whispered.

She grinned and stared into my eyes, tears still dripping out of hers, "I love you, too, same-same. I love you always."

I kissed her hand softly and passed out.

At two o'clock in the morning, the 105 howitzers at the A-camps of Ben Het and Dak Seang, along with the First Brigade, Fourth Infantry Division artillery at Dak To, lighted up a corridor through the mountains from Kontum to Dak Pek. A dust-off helicopter braved the dangerous rugged journey and flew into the valley of the Dak Pek to pick me up.

While I lay on a stretcher at the helipad in front of the dispensary, Ning held my hand, crying her eyes out. Too weak and unaware of what was happening, I didn't realize that seeing her crying hysterically as I was placed on the medevac was going to be the last time we would ever see each other.

Not too long after I was taken away, that night, to the 71st Evac Hospital in Pleiku, Ning boarded a C7A Caribou to go off and search for me in the big city. She was never seen again.

After a long time in hospitals in Vietnam, Japan, and the States, I was treated for falciparum malaria, the worst kind; methemoglobinemia, a blood disease; infectious hepatitis, dengue fever, anemia, and amoebic dysentery, all at once. At the same time, I was semicomatose and kept getting fevers of 108 degrees. I also got detoxified, realizing then that I had been an alcoholic since the age of fifteen. The Army, at Fort Bragg, gave me a three-profile medically, and I was not permitted to return to Vietnam.

The fight would have to be carried on for Dak Pek by others. My battles for the Montagnards and their plight would continue the rest of my life, but I was out of the fight for Dak Pek. I had been sabotaged by an enemy that couldn't lose.

6

De Oppresso Liber

THE SPECIAL FORCES MOTTO WAS, and is, *De Oppresso Liber.* In mid-1969, Staff Sergeant Joe Howard and Staff Sergeant Donald B. "Commo Willy" Williams got a chance to prove why that was the SF motto. The southeastern corner of Dak Pek's area of operations cornered near the NVA stronghold, the Tu Mrong Valley, and it apexed a triangle with twenty miles of jungled mountains to either Dak Seang to the southwest or Dak Pek to the northwest. No operations from Dak Pek had gone into that area for several years, so it was decided that the two NCOs would reconnoiter with twenty Montagnards from the tough recon platoon. Joe had left Dak Pek in late 1968, but returned in 1969, like most people, wanting to complete the job he had started.

The two men and their patrol were crammed onto two Huey helicopters at daybreak and whisked to the area of operations. The choppers touched down in an old mountain rice paddy that had been deserted some time before and was now overgrowing. Touched down was exactly what the choppers did, too. It was really more like touching the tops of weeds as they passed across the semiopen area while the twenty-two men jumped out, crashed and burned, and ran into the nearby tree line as quickly as possible. This was a "hot" area.

Both Joe and Commo Willy had been promoted to E-6 a year earlier, and Joe had about two weeks date-of-rank, so he was in charge of the operation. He sent a three-man point patrol out ahead of the main body and the twenty-two fighters moved slowly through the virgin territory.

They crossed a fast-running stream with beautiful jungle flowers growing along its banks. It cascaded down the side of a mountain and wasn't even shown on a map. It flowed into a wider stream that ran the length of the valley and flowed into the whitewater Dak Poko River. Overgrown Highway Fourteen, no longer a usable road for years, ran along its banks. The small patrol followed the tracks of a herd of wild pigs for a short distance and kept on the finger-line ridge they were climbing after their tracks dropped off the side.

The three point men were named Bip, Rok, and Blak, their names meaning respectively duck, cow, and cockroach. The Jeh believed that evil spirits could be warded away from your child if you gave him an ugly name, so most names translated into objects such as manure, vomit, rat, and so on. Bip was the most experienced warrior and the oldest, so he was in charge. He led the way as the three kept climbing, having been given only a general direction of travel by Joe Howard. The mountain was tall and kept getting steeper.

Something moved in the growth ahead of them. They dropped and listened. Whoever or whatever it was was only ten feet away, but the jungle in the mountains around Dak Pek was so thick that moving from here to over there was a three-day trip. The men eased their M-2 carbines out and lay on their stomachs. Each felt the sting of numerous mosquitoes. They waited.

The movement was still there, but no voices, no human sounds. Bip slowly, carefully, eased the barrel of his M-2 forward and pushed aside several branches. He moved them around, hooking them onto other branches, and finally saw the source of the noise, the side of a long, thick python.

He stood and smiled at the others, whispering, *"Klan."*

They moved forward and Rok, yanking out his long thick-bladed Jeh knife, swiftly decaptitated the twelve-foot-long snake. The men took several minutes to chop the thrashing snake into short sections and then went forward, chewing on python. The other pieces were left for their buddies who were several minutes behind them, to eat.

The patrol crossed over that mountain and went down the other side, crossed another stream running through a foliage- and vine-choked narrow valley, and started up the next ridge line. The point came to a well-used trail running along the ridge about twenty feet higher than the stream and stopped, waiting for the main body to catch up.

When the patrol caught up with the point, they examined the trail and saw that it was well used but invisible from aerial observation. Joe sent a man up the trail and another down the trail, and the patrol took a break in place.

Every break on an operation started the same; first everyone took a big swallow of water from his canteen. Joe and Commo Willy each took salt pills to replace the salt they had lost in sweat. Tieh, their interpreter, did the same. Next everyone lighted cigarettes, then pulled up his trouser legs. Each man in the patrol had at least ten big thick blood-filled leeches clinging to his calves and shins. A couple of the Jeh attached little gauze pads to a six-inch stick and applied a couple of drops of Army insect repellent. The rest, like the two Americans, just used the lighted ends of their cigarettes and applied them to the back of each leech. The little creature immediately backed its head out of the victim's skin and the man pulled it off. The three point men had to strip down to their loincloths and have friends remove leeches from all over their bodies. When they were lying down listening to the python moving about, numerous leeches dropped and climbed down their shirts.

Commo Willy said, "Why don't we go ahead and eat lunch?"

"Sure," Joe said. "Tell them to fix cold lunch. No fires, Tieh."

The interpreter passed it along and the little wiry men opened their packs and pulled out bags of indigenous rations—dried pieces of fish and seafood, rice, and vegetables.

Joe Howard opened up an LRP, or long-range-patrol, ration of chili con carne and Commo Willy decided on spaghetti. Each man opened plastic packs containing dehydrated ingredients and poured a canteen cup of water in, stirring it. Both NCOs, like most good SF NCOs in Vietnam, added a dash of hot sauce to their mix from a bottle Joe carried in his ruck. They ate quickly, pretending that the water they added was boiling.

Sergeant Williams, in the middle of a bite, stopped, spoon in his mouth, and stared at the trail's edge. Joe noticed the furrow in Commo Willy's brow and his eyes followed the other's line of sight. They both set their meals down and walked over to a spot five feet beyond Tieh, who was savoring a square of candy wrapped with edible rice paper that looked like plastic. They knelt down and examined a piece of thick bamboo along the trail. The problem was, it was not growing straight up and down like normal bamboo; it ran sideways along the side of the trail. The two men brushed away leaves and branches and saw that the bamboo ran all along the path, going underground. They moved along on their hands and knees and found the bamboo emerging from the ground again, but again, covered with sticks and leaves.

Commo Willy felt the pipe and said, "There's water running through it."

"Son of a bitch!" Joe said.

As if there had been a silent signal, all the Montagnards, as one, dropped their food and picked up their rifles. They each picked up wrappers, cigarette butts, and any sign of their passing. Joe and Don had been around the Yards long enough to know that these men sensed when the enemy was in the area and headed toward them. The two sergeants gave hand signals and the Yards moved into the jungle in an L-shaped ambush formation. Joe Howard and Commo Willy separated and lay one-third and two-thirds of the way down the line. There was activity, laughing, and joking one minute; one minute later there was relative silence.

Each man listened to the sounds of dozens of mosquitoes, straining to hear the sounds of an enemy. *Bark!* Everyone jumped, then relaxed when the sound was identified as that of a barking deer nearby. Far off, a B-52 carpet-bombing strike went in somewhere, sounding like a busy bowling alley some distance away, maybe at the jungle's edge.

Commo Willy almost heard the sound of a telegraph key. Like a person going to bed after starting to learn how to play PacMan and seeing little yellow munching monsters, he sometimes heard the steady chattering of a telegraph, after getting away from the radio room. Commo Willy spent hour after hour seated in front of the big single-side band radio, twelve feet under layers of dirt, rocks, PSP, and reinforced concrete, placed there to protect the team's commo room and TOC from incoming 120 rockets. The communications was the lifeblood of the A-team and Sergeant Williams worked hour after hour, building still another backup underground antenna, reinforcing a generator bunker, and doing a myriad of busy things; but always one ear at least was monitoring the Sierra Sierra Bravo, while another ear was listening for an operation to call in on the ground-to-ground frequency on the Prick 25, and still another ear would be tuned into the air-to-ground Prick 25 listening for the sounds of any incoming aircraft. Had he been a descendant of Vincent van Gogh instead of Theodore Reik, life would have been unsettling.

Flap, flap, flap . . . the unmistakable sound of hardened feet on hardened trail. Everyone tensed. A gray-haired Montagnard woman, dirty breasts drooping after years of work, padded nonchalantly down the trail, a woven basket full of rice balanced expertly on her head. Directly behind her walked another rice carrier, but this one was a wide-eyed girl of twelve years. They both almost fell over as the patrol jumped out and surrounded them.

As soon as the two women got over the initial shock, both started chatting incessantly to every Jeh man within sight. The patrol members seemed to smile, got excited, and inched the yakking, happy females to Tieh. Joe and Don stared in openmouthed wonder as the group chattered on. Several strikers walked up and handed the two women pieces of candy.

Excited and grinning broadly, Tieh finally turned to the two Americans and explained, *"Trung-si,* that old woman is grandmother to the girl. Four years ago, their village at Dak Pek. You know Dak Dru Doc?"

"Which one is that?" Commo Willy asked.

Joe said, "Remember the one that got overrun by NVA last year, the one up north across the river?"

"Yeah," Commo Willy replied.

Tieh continued enthusiastically, "Yes, and it got overrun four years ago. Many villagers were killed. *Beaucoups.* Everybody runs into jungle. This old lady and her granddaughter were captured by the NVA. They make them work near here for four years."

Commo Willy and Joe Howard got excited and slapped each other on the arm.

"Are you shittin' us, Tieh?" Williams asked.

"Huh?" Tieh replied. "Oh, no *Trung-si* Williams, I'm very sure. Their family be *beaucoups* happy. That man, Ek, is her nephew. Their family thinks both women dead all these years. There will be big celebration."

Joe Howard said, "Tieh, ask if they were the only prisoners."

"I did, *Trung-si* Joe Howard. There are more Jeh

from Dak Pek who are prisoners, too. Twenty-five, maybe," Tieh said.

Joe and Willy looked at each other, broad smiles on their faces.

Joe continued talking to the woman and the young girl, through Tieh, and Commo Willy, in the meantime, called Dak Pek for choppers.

After Commo Willy got off the horn, Joe said, "Man, we need to saddle up and get them out of here. The NVA position is just a quarter mile down the trail. We'll get out of the area and have them extracted and I'm going to get us some reinforcements brought in and we'll go kick some ass."

"Yeah!" was Commo Willy's enthusiastic reply.

The patrol policed the area to insure there was no sign of their passing, and they withdrew several kilometers over the ridge line to an old mountain rice field. Before dark the two Montagnard females were on a Huey helicopter on their way to Dak Pek and a contingent of eighty more Montagnards were on the ground, under the command of Staff Sergeant Howard. The operation moved slightly away from the area and set up a perimeter in the thick jungle. They would wait until morning.

The next morning the Dak Pek strike force was ready to move at first light.

Joe Howard and Don Williams wore their normal operation uniform, the "tiger suit," and Commo Willy wore the floppy camo hat. Joe, a Texas cowboy, however, wore his normal black Stetson hat he wore on all operations. This endeared the Montagnards to him even more, because they just loved American cowboys.

Joe and Don were both in their mid-twenties. Joe was thin and had black hair and moustache. Don, on the other hand, had blond hair and the All-American boyish look.

Both men were very well liked by the Jeh, which was important on an operation, and both were definitely SF.

The enemy was nearby, and they were ready to seek him out and destroy him wherever they could find him.

An hour later Joe called the first break, and it seemed as if every man on the operation had to urinate and void his bowels. There is a psychological condition in man, in which he voids his body's wastes when he senses that he is about to go into battle. Maybe it's nature's way of lightening the load. This is the reason that entertainers, or speakers, will sometimes vomit or develop diarrhea before performing.

They arrived at the spot in the trail where the two women were found and discovered no sign of any others passing. The point cautiously moved down the trail. It has been told that the Montagnards performed similarly elsewhere, but the strikers from Dak Pek definitely had a sense about them to detect the enemy. On an operation they would walk down the jungle trails or follow the point chopping with machetes. Most of the time these dynamic little warriors laughed, talked, told war stories, and thought about food. When they got near the enemy, no signal was ever given; all the Montagnards just knew that the enemy was near. They got quiet, walked slowly, all senses on the alert, and carried their weapons in a ready position. They knew the enemy was close.

The trail wound downhill on a slight angle and turned back toward the north into a narrow jungle-filled draw. The operation stopped. The Yards immediately and automatically took up defensive positions along the trail, facing in all directions. Vietnam was not a gentlemen's war and their were no front lines. The true front line was simply the edge of each man's own personal vulnerability.

They moved forward slowly and the two Americans caught up with the point, who had halted and let the operation catch up, folding around it into a defensive perimeter. In front of Commo Willy and Joe Howard were several rows of little rice hooches, each made of woven bamboo and covered with a camouflaged thatched roof, invisible to aerial observation. Each hooch contained a very large earthenware crock, a couple feet across, four feet tall, and filled to the brim with mountain-grown rice. There was literally enough rice to feed an army. Several fires were burning and there were also ten bamboo hooches that were being lived in.

This veritable supply depot and inhabited location was over twenty miles from any known human population area. It was well hidden away in the middle of some very thick jungle. Each hooch was equipped with a trap door and escape tunnel under it.

The men walked around and surveyed the storage area. There was rice everywhere, and it had all been grown, under the eyes of American technology, but hidden from those electronics by layer after layer of jungle leaves.

While Commo Willy called the incredible find into Dak Pek, Joe took a patrol and searched for a suitable spot to start clearing a landing zone. There was a flat space, another overgrown rice field less than an eighth of a mile down another trail. He had a team of strikers start hacking away with their machetes and returned to the enemy location. Commo Willy made arrangements for a helicopter to come in from Dak To, a half-hour flight about due south.

A platoon secured the helicopter landing zone while the rest of the operation set up a perimeter around the enemy location. Joe sent a couple of fire-team-size patrols out as an early warning against any NVA traveling down any of the trails coming into the area. The hidden bamboo pipe started at a cascading mountain waterfall and ended at the village, a constant source of fresh water for them without having to expose themselves going to a river or stream.

A chopper flew in and was greeted by Commo Willy. He and a handful of Yards hopped on and were given a palletful of sandbags. They jumped down, waved off the chopper, divided the bags, and carried them to the village. There a detail started filling sandbags with rice and carried the bags back to the LZ. This continued for a number of hours, but it was not making much of a dent.

With night approaching, Joe and Commo Willy halted the rice-bagging operation, moved people into night defensive positions, and set up ambush patrols. Patrols that went out during the day found tons of enemy sign, so the two NCOs were anxious to see if they could pop anything that night.

The First Brigade of the Fourth Infantry Division, headquartered at Dak To, operated all over this area, quite often on joint operations with Dak Pek and sister A-camps like Ben Het, Dak Seang, Plei Jrang, Mang Buk, and Polei Kleng. They sent numerous night ambushes out but seldom were successful in springing them. Joe Howard knew why. The Fourth Division ambushes were always put out on major trails, which does seem like reasonable tactics. The NVA, however, didn't pay much attention to what the textbooks said they were supposed to do.

Joe sent out six ambush patrols; two were set up on major trails coming into the area of operations, and the other four were set up on major streams in the area, which were shallow enough to walk in.

The night was pitch-black. One of the trail ambushes was on a major trail that ran east and west and came down off the ridge that pointed at the ruins of the former A-camp of Dak Sut. Six Montagnards were on the ambush, which was set up right next to the trail, with each one directly behind a tree for cover.

Nguyen Van Tho was born in Vinh, North Vietnam, in February 1947, right after the start of Tet. He was a member of the 24th NVA Regiment (formerly the 66th) of the Second NVA Division. His father had died a year and a half earlier for Ho Chi and the cause. His dad killed two American GIs in the midst of the confusion of the 1968 Tet Offensive in Da Nang. Dad hid in a cave, his unit's staging area, in Marble Mountain, until the time came to move out. Tho's father ran up to the first two Americans he saw when he entered the city. They had shocked looks on their faces, and one even tried to pull out a .45 automatic, too late. Tho's dad squeezed the detonator in his right hand, which detonated the American Claymore mine that was wired to his chest under his black pajamas. The back blast killed the martyr instantly, but it also spread parts of the two American soldiers over half a city block.

His dad was a dead sapper, but he was a living memory in the mind of Tho, a memory to be revered. Tho didn't know if he would die, too, but he knew that he would die hard. With his squad he carefully padded up a trail that ran east away from the deserted *Luc Luong Dak Biet* camp that had been called Dak Sut.

His footsteps, like those of his comrades, were silent. The sandals he wore were cut from the tires of an L-19 aircraft that was shot down two weeks earlier in the area west of Kontum, near the Plei Trap Valley but a little south. They were cut to size and then straps were cut from the thin rubber in the sidewalls and were wedged, with a knife blade, through the slits cut into the bottom edges of the sandals.

The patrol moved carefully along with the orders to locate and probe the perimeter of the CIDG operation from Dak Pek. They were to make the probe in order to get the Imperialist forces to fire their automatic weapons. The men were to make a sketch of the automatic weapons positions, along with other intelligence data they could gather, and rejoin their unit as quickly as possible.

The previous day a trail watcher fired two shots from his SKS rifle and the information was relayed to headquarters that he had spotted a platoon-size unit walking across the major trail intersection he overlooked. Had he fired one shot, it would have meant a squad-size unit, and three shots would have meant company size or larger. One minute after the trail watcher's original shots, he fired another single shot. This indicated that the unit he spotted traveled north on the trail. Two quick shots would have been east, two spaced shots meant south, and three fast shots meant west. Sometimes the NVA and VC didn't have radar or radios, but they had effective communications and enemy surveillance procedures anyway. A recon squad was quickly dispatched to the area and spotted the women being extracted by helicopter and the reinforcements arriving. The old woman and the girl were recognized as two from the labor gangs that worked the rice fields.

An army doesn't necessarily travel on its stomach, especially the NVA and VC. Dedicated to a cause and a reason to fight, as they were, an army will sometimes go for long periods without food and still carry on the fight. At some distinct point, though, the men just starve to death if they have no food supply. The rice supply was a major food source for the 24th Regiment and other units of the Second Division, and it was definitely in jeopardy. The decision was made that the food stores were going to be very costly to the Americans, if they had to be sacrificed.

Nguyen Van Tho and his comrades moved toward the American perimeter at a fast but careful pace. It was Tho's turn at point for the patrol when he heard the almost inaudible cough. He raised his left hand straight up, warning his partners to halt, and then lowered it as he and his buddies melted silently into the shadows of the night, listening to the incessant sounds of the jungle. Tho turned and moved silently back to his squad leader, *Trung-si* Thieu. Crawling on his belly, he slithered across the trail with no perceptible noise. This was due to the hours and hours his proud father had spent teaching him how to slither quickly through concertina barbed wire without getting caught and all cut up.

"Rinh," Tho said to his boss, indicating an ambush.

"Nem da," Thieu whispered, telling him to throw stones.

Tho nodded in the dark, turned, and slid away, whispering the orders to the other squad members.

Everyone knew what to do.

Tho would be the one with the dangerous reconnoiter, as he was the one with the most skill at it. He left his AK-47, pack, and harness with his buddy and crawled toward the sound of the cough. His movements became so slow that it looked as if he wasn't even moving. His body glided along the trail, so low that the cloth of his black pajamas touched the ground the full length of his body, but he was moving forward supported by the taut muscles in his arms and legs, resembling a Komodo dragon in his appearance.

Twenty minutes and fifteen feet later, he reached up and touched the end of the barrel of an M-2 carbine. He moved on to the next position and located the man by one sliver of barrel shine from the moonlight sneaking in through cracks in the thick triple canopy above. It took Tho an hour to move carefully along and locate the exact position of each of the six men in the ambush.

He also located the two Claymore mines that were placed along the trail near the center of the ambush, along with the commo wire that ran back to the two men in charge of them. He seriously considered cutting through the wires, stealing the antipersonnel mines and using them on the hapless patrol, but instead he chose to use his usual tactic of turning the mines around so they faced the Montagnard strikers.

As ordered, Tho and his buddies were going to crawl forward, out of the killing zone of the ambush, and toss stones at the patrol. Hiding behind trees, they knew that the upset Americans would detonate their Claymores first, killing at least the two setting them off. They would watch the muzzle flashes of the frightened soldiers and simply plink them off by firing aimed shots above the flashes.

There was one problem in Thieu and Tho's carefully orchestrated plan that had been carried off so many times before. The recon squad that watched the choppers from a distance could not tell that the soldiers were Jeh strikers from Dak Pek, so the Second Division G-2 assumed they were Fourth Division troops. Tho didn't know, when he carefully and skillfully sneaked along the ambush and located each man and position, that the men he was scouting were Montagnards. The Montagnard strikers watched him as he scouted their locations and turned the Claymores around. In fact, when Bayh started to detonate his Claymore in Tho's face, his older brother gently grabbed his arm and gave it an imperceptible squeeze.

Like shadows, the NVA patrol glided along the black muddy trail toward the ambush location, and Tho carefully placed each man behind individual trees across from the killing zone. He would start the pebble throwing and would take the first shot with his AK. That had always worked in the past.

The men were in place and Tho stood up slowly, behind his tree. He took a stone out of his left hand and lifted his right. He aimed at the spot he had picked out between the two Claymores and threw the rock. It hit a tree trunk with a thud and the two Claymores went off, except that they were in the darkness behind the NVA patrol.

Suddenly the Montagnard guns started chattering, but not from the positions in front of the patrol. Instead, they came from the branches of the big trees above and behind the squad of NVA soldiers.

Trung-si Thieu, of his entire squad, was able to fire off two rounds, but only into the ground at his feet. He felt his face hit the ground, shortly after the bullets and wondered why he couldn't fire back at the stupid American Imperialists.

Nguyen Van Tho got his wish: he died a hero like his father before him, but he didn't die hard. His body was torn into numerous pieces and slammed into the bark of the tree he thought he was hiding behind. He did start to hear the explosions of the Claymores, or maybe it was just sound caused by his brain exploding.

The entire squad was a patrol that would be wondered about the next morning. Their CO would wonder if they *Chieu Hoied,* got captured, killed, or just *di di maued* toward the nearest town. The patrol of Montagnards from Dak Pek slipped silently down the trail, away from the main body of troops, and set up a new ambush, hoping to surprise another patrol coming to check on *Trung-si* Thieu's hapless unit.

Five miles away, six more Dega from Dak Pek lay along the banks of a stream that headwatered at a cascading waterfall coming off a ridge line bordering the Tu Mrong Valley. The clear stream ran swiftly downhill into another, which ran into another that poured into the Dak Poko due east of Dak Seang.

Jal was the squad leader, and he rested his chin on the butt of his rifle as he and his men waited for some NVA to move silently down the noisy stream. He thought he saw some movement upstream and strained his eyes, his heart pounding in anticipation of battle.

Tiu was the only man in his squad he was concerned about, as it was the young man's first operation. Jal had been in battle with all the others in the squad and knew they would perform courageously, but Tiu was a different story. He thought about it. Tiu was from a neighboring village, Dak Peng Sial Peng, and Jal knew the man's late father, a true warrior who had been killed on an operation with *Trung-uy* Bendell not far from here. Tiu was a young man, thirteen summers in age, but he had a wife, and he was responsible. Jal decided not to worry.

Tiu thought he heard something beyond Jal, and his heart pounded in anticipation of battle. He wanted battle.

He wanted it badly. Tiu's father had died not far from here while fighting in a fierce battle with *Trung-uy* Bendell, and his dad had died bravely, very bravely. The tall American came to his mother after the battle and told her how brave his father had been. She cried for hours afterward, but she was so proud. He would fight as if his father were fighting next to him. In fact, Tiu believed that his dad's spirit was there with him. He was a Christian and so was his late father. He knew his dad was now with Jesus, as the missionaries taught them. He would never bring shame to his family. If fighting started and he was scared, Tiu decided he would be the only one to know of his fear. If shot, he would not cry out. If captured, he would spit in the enemy's face and laugh at them, even if they killed him. His wife was with child and his son or daughter would carry his family forward anyway.

A sound again. Some movement to the right, and Jal's eyes moved slowly, focusing on an NVA soldier standing in the middle of the rushing water. The man had his hand raised and was moving it slowly forward, signaling to those following. He took several cautious steps and a second soldier appeared, the red star on his pith helmet clearly visible in the moonlight.

Tiu felt his throat tighten, and he tried to swallow, but he couldn't. There was no saliva. He wanted to urinate but controlled himself. He knelt and moved his hand slowly in front of his position, searching, as he watched the patrol move slowly down the stream. At their speed, it would be ten minutes before the whole patrol was in the killing zone of his ambush. His fingers found a pebble and he cleaned it by rubbing his thumb across it several times. He inched it up to his mouth and slipped it between his lips. Tiu worked the pebble around in his mouth and his saliva started flowing again. He would have to put off being frightened until later, he decided, for now he had work to do.

Jal moved his hand slowly along the stock of his M-2 carbine and flipped the selector switch on automatic. The second man down from him was Plem and he was using a BAR, a Browning automatic rifle, and that man could shoot. Jal knew that he must start the ambush, and his mind went through all that the Americans had taught him. They must shoot low, because there is a tendency to fire too high in the dark. They would fire the first magazine on full auto and lay down a heavy volume of fire. The second magazine would be fired on semiautomatic, and he would pick out targets and aim at them. He controlled his breathing and relaxed.

A noise to the left. The NVA froze in midstream. Something was in the trees directly across the stream. A shadow moved under the branches and Jal gulped heavily, wondering what unforeseen danger lurked, just a stone's throw away.

A tiger stepped from the shadows into the moonlight and started across the stream, headed directly at Jal. Jal froze. When he was seven years old, Jal had been out in the mountain rice fields, and he and several villagers watched in horror while a tiger came out of the jungle, attacked and killed his mother, and dragged her into the jungle to eat her.

Jal's heart pounded. He couldn't move. The NVA trained their AK-47s on the tiger as it started up the bank, headed right for Jal. They couldn't see a thing because his patrol was carefully hidden in the jungle blackness. The breeze blew from the tiger to Jal, but soon the big cat would be upon him, and he couldn't move. Closer it came, and closer still. He could almost touch it. The big cat stopped and let out a mighty roar, the moonlight shining off the wet orange-and-black hairs on his side. Jal could smell him. The ambush would be compromised, but Jal couldn't move. The tiger made another step and Jal fought to keep from whimpering or screaming. Something had to be done, but he was paralyzed with fear.

A figure silently launched itself onto the ground beside Jal and an arm flew forward. A stick hit the tiger in the snout, and it turned with a roar. It slowly turned and walked back into the stream and headed toward the NVA patrol. They didn't move.

Jal turned his head and stared into the smiling face of young Tiu, lying next to him. He reached over and gave the young man's hand a squeeze, and they smiled at each other in the darkness.

The tiger moved up onto the bank, not seeing the motionless NVA. It walked upstream along the far bank and was soon gone from sight.

Less careful about ambushes now, the NVA patrol moved more rapidly down the stream, all nervously looking back to insure the tiger wasn't doubling back. Jal had no problem with paralysis when they reached the killing zone. All the NVA went down in a wave, except one. As soon as the ambush opened up, he dropped straight down, went underwater, and swam downstream in the waist-deep water. Tiu didn't even wait. Knife in his mouth, he scrambled down the bank, dived in, and took off down the tributary himself. The patrol couldn't watch for him, as they concentrated on the NVA soldier who stood up in front of them, blood pumping from a shoulder wound. He walked forward smiling and raised his good arm.

"Chieu hoi, Amereecan! Chieu hoi! No sweat!" he yelled, fear in his voice, as he spouted the words meaning he wanted to come over to Saigon's side.

Jal and the other patrol members stood up and walked to the water's edge, weapons pointed at the man. He saw they were Montagnards, and his eyes opened wide in horror.

"Moi!" was all he could say. This was the Vietnamese equivalent of the word "nigger."

They all grinned and opened up on automatic. His bloody corpse flew backward into the fast-moving water.

A scream downstream turned them all to the left, and they saw the other NVA soldier stand straight up on his toes, head turned toward the sky in a primal scream. His hands clutched at something sticking in his stomach. Tiu came up out of the water, his right hand twisting the handle of his big knife, which was buried to the hilt in the enemy soldier's stomach. Tiu grabbed the man's lapel, pulled his face close, and grinned into the man's widened eyes. The NVA died, his body slipping off the blade of the Bowie-size knife, and slid into the cold, clear stream.

Two other ambushes were sprung that night and the Jeh warriors returned to the mother unit early the next day, tired but excited from the night's battle.

The deaths of the NVA could not be officially counted with American spot reports or after-action reports, because no American physically saw the NVA bodies or witnessed their deaths. How many similar patrols had been successfully carried out like that by Montagnards trained and led by the Special Forces, but whose success could not be reported? Countless.

Joe Howard and Commo Willy were awakened at first light to a blazing fire near their hammocks. Two Montagnards had brought the Americans canteen cups and boiled water in them. Joe prepared scalding hot coffee and Commo Willy opted for hot cocoa. They prepared breakfast from LRP rations while Tieh translated the patrol leader's reports to Joe.

Commo Willy related a story about his most recent trip to Kontum while they ate.

"I laid down on this wooden-frame bunk in that big EM barracks. You know which one I mean? Near B-24 compound?" Don said.

"Yeah, I know," Joe said, lighting a cigarette and stirring a new packet of instant coffee into his water.

"This E-4 from the Fourth Division is cleaning his M-16 in the bunk next to me, and I decide to lay down for a fucking nap, okay," Commo Willy went on. "All of a sudden, boom. This fucking gun goes off and the bullet shatters the frame of my cot one inch above my head."

Joe said, "Kick his ass?"

"No, but he thought I was going to," the blond sergeant continued. "You should have seen his face. I put on my beret, picked up my piece and my war bag, and walked to the end of the barracks, lay down on another bunk, and went to sleep."

Joe started laughing. "Son of a bitch, Commo Willy, you went to fucking sleep?"

"He thought I did. Like to have shit himself," Don said and both men laughed.

Joe started to take a sip of coffee and stopped the cup at his lips, "Tastes best if you can lay your bayonet on it and it floats."

He started to sip the black brew and a rifle cracked from the nearby jungle and the cup flew sideways from the sergeant's hand. Everyone near the fire hit the ground and scrambled for rifles.

Joe grabbed his M-16 and whipped it up and started firing, while yelling, "You fucked up my canteen cup! You asshole!"

"I'll take the right side," Commo Willy yelled above the roar of weapons.

Joe gave him the okay sign and moved to his left on his belly as a tremendous volley of fire rained on his operation from the nearby jungle. Commo Willy moved to the right and started directing Montagnards into fighting positions behind trees and in depressions. The fire fight was deafening, and it seemed the NVA were everywhere, pouring fire in on the Dak Pek strikers.

Commo Willy made it to the radio and called for a FAC out of Dak To. He got a quick response from one already airborne, flying VR for an operation southwest of Dak Seang.

The man was there within ten minutes, flying an O-1 aircraft. The NVA volume of fire slowed down a little.

"Boston Pencil Alpha, Bird Dog One-four, over," the voice crackled over the Prick 25.

"One-four, Alpha," Commo Willy answered. "Glad you're here. We're taking a lot of small-arms fire from the south and west, over."

"Yeah, I think I got an eyeball on them. You spread out on both side of the thick draw, over?"

"Rog-O," Commo Willy said. "The firing's picking up. You got anybody on the way, over?"

"Standby, over," the pilot replied.

Commo Willy said, "Standing by."

Seconds later, the voice crackled again. "Okay, Alpha, got you a couple of Spads on station and some Victor November pilots, over."

"They fight better from planes than on the ground, over?" Williams asked.

The FAC laughed over the radio and said, "I'll let 'em show you. Give me a smoke, over."

Commo Willy looked across the trail at Joe, behind a small clump of trees. He gave him the grenade signal, and Joe threw out a yellow smoke grenade. The smoke curled out and worked its way toward the jungle canopy. It hung over the leaves and finally started filtering up into the bright sunshine. The FAC's plane buzzed directly overhead.

"I see yellow, over," his cheery voice said.

"Affirmative, over," Commo Willy replied.

"Big Rog, gonna put a marking round on the bad guys and then watch these VN pilots do their thing. They trained in the States, you know, over?"

"Okay, we'll watch, over."

The O-1 went up into the sky, made a tight turn, and dived toward the NVA lines. There was a streaking sound and a rocket shot out from under the plane and a Willy Peter (white phosphorous) round landed squarely in the middle of the NVA line. A giant plume of white smoke poured skyward and Commo Willy listened to the screams of an NVA soldier who was apparently burned by the hot jellylike substance on his skin.

Out of the clouds streaked a propeller-driven World War II vintage Spad airplane, spouting angry bursts of twenty mike-mike from his cannons. He looked as if he would crash right into the NVA unit but pulled the plane out of the dive, at the very last second, and Commo Willy saw two napalm canisters drop from under the plane's wings. Flames shot up in a long line and more NVA screams were heard.

Commo Willy's eyes flashed over to Joe Howard and saw the cowboy sergeant grinning broadly. The NVA fire stopped completely. Joe winked at Don Williams.

A second Spad came straight down out of the low-hanging clouds and spit out more cannon fire. He too dropped two more napalm canisters, part of which fried the western side of the NVA unit. As soon as he pulled up, the first one was there again and dropped a CBU canister. Hundreds of cluster-bomb units rained down on the NVA position, exploding with a staccato-sounding blast.

By the time the air strike ended, Joe Howard had a line of strikers up behind trees and ready to assault on-line. He sent one detachment of hardened fighters downhill to act as a blocking force in case the NVA crossed over the ravine and tried to withdraw down the main east/ west trail. After Commo Willy signaled him that the Spads were done with the air strike, Joe sent his strikers forward on line and assaulted the NVA position, but there was no return fire.

The NVA had withdrawn quickly and completely. There were numerous blood pools on the ground and pieces of uniforms and weapons.

The operation went back to filling up bags of rice and prepared them to be loaded on incoming choppers. Hueys came in twice and took bags of rice out, but they couldn't carry enough, so a big Chinook was sent in from Dak To.

Commo Willy had the platoon of Yards with him expand the landing zone, which had been cut in a horseshoe shape. The Chinook set down in the LZ, which looked like a giant green patch of overgrown beard stubble, with little sharp bamboo roots sticking up into the air. Commo Willy and several Jeh climbed up the tailgate and started loading bags of rice inside the steel bowels of the giant airship.

Crackackackack! Whumpumpumpumpump! Clangangangang! Automatic weapons fire cracked past the open tailgate: a series of bullets nosed into the skin of the craft. The rotors whirred to life, and the big helicopter prepared to take off.

The crew chief, miked with the cockpit, yelled to Commo Willy, "We're taking fire! Small arms!"

The Montagnard on the craft with Commo Willy was taking bags at the tailgate and handing them to the American, so he saw the others scrambling for the protective cover of the jungle. He was now just a few steps behind the others.

The chopper started to lift off and Commo Willy grabbed his M-16 and took a running dive off the back end. He hit the ground on his chest and a sharp bamboo root that was sticking up tore the skin off the left side of his ribcage. The downdraft from the lifting Chinook pushed him almost into the ground, and bullets chattered over his head from two directions.

He raised his head, squinting against the dirt and debris being raised by the prop wash. Hundreds of lights, the firing of weapons, blinked along the edge of the giant horseshoe. A contingent of NVA had lined up in the trees just south of the LZ and were firing at the CIDG. Commo Willy felt like an ant sitting on top of a golf ball.

The sound of the retreating helicopter was now drowned out by the deafening roar of battle. Commo

Willy saw dirt and pieces of bamboo flying up in the air all around him, from the small-arms fire being aimed at him. He felt more naked and exposed than at any time before in his life. The Montagnards were laying down a heavy volume of fire and were very ferocious fighters, but some were not exactly candidates for the All-Asia Olympic marksmanship team.

He crawled toward the north end of the horseshoe, but more bullets kicked up dirt in front of him as he tried to crawl across a slightly elevated section. Commo Willy hugged the dirt and realized he was pinned down. The Dega started yelling, maybe to encourage him, or maybe because they were totally psyched.

Sergeant Williams was getting pissed. Like most career SFers, he had a distinct dislike of being shot at. It was disrespectful. He reached up on his harness and yanked out his sheath knife, which was upside down on the left shoulder strap. He cut the olive-drab tape that was wrapped around the red smoke grenade attached to the front of his right shoulder strap. Commo Willy pulled the pin on the grenade, let the flipper fly, and threw it toward the enemy soldiers. The Montagnards started yelling even louder and increased their already heavy volume of fire. His side was bleeding and burned painfully, but he saw fewer clumps of dirt and bamboo being hit around him as the red smoke obscured the NVA's view of the LZ.

"Fuck you Commie bastards!" he screamed as he jumped up into a crouch, threw a high-explosive grenade at the NVA position, and ran for the edge of the LZ.

He hit the tree line, amid the cheers of the Montagnards, and dived over a log along the jungle's edge, tumbling ass over tin cans into the undergrowth. Behind him he heard the sound of an airplane between the numerous bursts of weapons fire. He scrambled to his feet and looked out at the sky above the NVA position. An O-1 just going into a dive fired a rocket into the

NVA line, a Willy Peter marking around. Commo Willy looked around quickly and saw Joe Howard speaking into the Prick 25 at another end of the horseshoe-shaped LZ. Green smoke swirled up behind him, and he gave the radio operator a little wave.

A minute later an F-4 came screaming out of the sky and arced back into a dive barely above the trees. Flames of hell exploded along the lines of enemy infantry as napalm erupted in their midst. The targeting was so accurate that screams could be heard above the sound of gunfire. No sooner had the napalm canisters exploded along the jungle's edge than a second jet suddenly appeared, pulling out of its dive, and two 500-pound bombs sent NVA body parts flying everywhere. The FAC had the jets expend all of their ordinance on the fleeing enemy as they took off again toward the south.

Joe worked his way over to Commo Willy, after sending a BDA patrol out to do bomb damage assessment. The two shook hands and humped with the rest of the Yards back to the main perimeter.

They decided that the gulley their perimeter encompassed was just too dangerous to defend, so they moved the perimeter up above it on the hill overlooking it to the north. There they set up strong defensive positions for the evening and prepared for a vicious assault, but it never came. The NVA apparently had suffered enough, thanks to the US Air Force.

The next morning an early patrol reported to Joe Howard and asked him and Commo Willy to come down into the ravine quickly. They grabbed their gear and ten Yards and went down the hill. The first five four-foot-tall crocks, which had been filled to the rim with rice, were gone.

Joe said, "They must have wanted rice pretty bad to take a risk like that."

"Yeah, well I don't know about you, Joe, but I'm sick

and tired of trying to get this shit out of here," Commo Willy said.

"Amen to that," Joe replied. "Let's do something about it."

"Fucking A tweetybird!" Don replied.

Five hours later, the bomb-damage assessment patrol, headed by Commo Willy, reported in to Joe.

"That FAC got his boys right in there with the napalm. There isn't a fucking unburned leaf in that draw. They napalmed the shit out of that rice. It's all destroyed," Commo Willy said.

"Out-fucking-standing!" Joe replied. "Let's go home. It's a long walk to Dak Pek."

The Fall

ALL THE COMMUNIST SPIES at Dak Pek had turned in their information and reports for months— years, in some cases. All the signs started to fall into place.

It was February of 1970, almost a year after I was medevacked. Sergeant Weeks, the heavy-weapons NCO when I arrived, had been promoted to master sergeant and came back as the team Operations Sergeant. Joe Howard was gone. I was a captain at Bragg.

One of the first signs that the end was near was Hazel. After working at Dak Pek for six years, she finally quit, suddenly and without apparent reason.

SOG, which stood for Studies and Observation Group, had changed its name to Command and Control and was referred to as CCN for North, CCS for South, and CCC for Central. It was a top secret unit and was targeted by Hanoi for some of their most intensive intelligence gathering.

Hazel didn't open her new Kontum whorehouse in a spot where it would attract numerous customers. She didn't open it where it would make the most sense to open it, business-wise. Hazel opened her whorehouse about three hundred feet from the front gate to the CCC compound headquarters.

Shortly before, Mr. Bon, the head of the security platoon, went out on a local operation. The Dak Pek unit walked along a finger-line ridge, within spitting distance of where all the local VC were to surrender to me almost one year before. What Bon's operation didn't know was that an NVA patrol happened to be walking along the same ridge line, but several feet over from the Dak Pek patrol. One of the NVA point men spotted Bon, raised a B-40 rocket launcher, and fired. The rocket hit the tree next to Bon and exploded. A piece of shrapnel entered Bon's upper thigh and severed his femoral artery. It was very unusual for Bon to go out on an operation, but once every year or two he did go out on brief patrols or operations, probably for the sake of appearance. Ironically, days before the camp was supposed to be overrun, he bled to death on a ridge line overlooking the camp.

Commo Willy had been born in Virginia and spent his childhood there; then he and his mother moved to Florida after his graduation. In 1970 Staff Sergeant Williams had already been in Vietnam over three years, while many of his school classmates back in "the World" had graduated from college not long before and were embarking on their careers. He first served with the First Calvary Division and then went over to the Fifth Special Forces Group.

It was very important that Commo Willy was serving on a remote SF A-team and that he had spent over three years in a row in combat. Commo Willy had a personal goal that was more important to him than anything else. Commo Willy's father had been killed during World War II. His uncles and cousins had also been killed during World War II and Korea. His grandfather had been killed in combat, as well as all of his granduncles, too. In fact, the only male member of Commo Willy's family who had not been killed in combat was his great-grandfather: he was a mortician. Commo Willy had one personal mission, and that was to prove to his mother, grandmother, aunts, and female cousins that there was not a curse on the men in his family. He would go through the worst hells that Vietnam had to offer and come out of it alive.

The North Vietnamese Army had different plans for Staff Sergeant Donald B. "Commo Willy" Williams and the other Americans at the A-camp of Dak Pek, ODA-242.

When the attack came, it came suddenly, explosively and unexpectedly, and in the middle of the night. Targets had long since been identified and planned. Each NVA sapper had been given specific targets to hit, and hit they did.

It was about two o'clock in the morning and the NVA sappers were given the signal to climb out of the Dak Poko and infiltrate the camp. Ky carried three satchel charges and a detailed sketch of the targets he was to hit. A lump in his throat, but excited that he was serving the cause of the mighty Ho Chi Minh and the revolution, he passed into the enemy camp. A number of men met Ky and the other sappers at the camp's front gate. He was told that several had been members of the LLDB team in the camp, and he assumed they were the ones who had slit the throats of the guards lying across the barrier, which was now next to him. Other VC infiltrators in the camp had already cut the detonator wires going to Claymores around the American hill, and they smiled at Ky as he trotted by, following a man who had been the payroll master for Dak Pek's strike force.

Bon was a hero as far as spies went, and this man had shared Bon's bunker. During the two years he spent at Dak Pek, he pinpointed numerous targets, which he was directing the sappers to now. He looked at Ky's sketch and pointed at the three targets he had been assigned: Nhual's bunker and the two radio towers. Ky moved to them quickly and placed the charges against each target. That was all he had to do, until all the satchel charges in the camp exploded simultaneously. Ky unslung his AK-47 and headed for the dispensary. He would climb on top of it and wait to snipe at targets of opportunity. He looked around at his thousands of shadowy comrades.

The NVA infiltrators swept silently through paths cut

through the barbed wire and through the gates. They went to pre-assigned positions and planted more satchel charges of explosives. Besides the bases of Commo Willy's two large radio towers and Nhual's bunker door, they also placed explosives at the door of every American's bunker, the American hill's four-deuce mortars and .50 caliber machine guns, the American TOC, commo room, emergency medical bunker, ammo bunkers, the camp 105 howitzers, LLDB team house, American team house, interpreters' bunkers, and many other important targets.

All the satchel charges had synchronized timing detonators on them. In the meantime, other sappers carrying satchel charges with fuses got into position, ready to deliver their deadly packages after the timed explosions went off. Still more were to throw their charges on targets of opportunity. Even more sappers, carrying infantry weapons, sat poised just outside the camp, ready to sweep over it in waves after the initial attack. Some carried ladders to throw across the giant punji-stake-filled tank trap and others carried bangalore torpedoes to toss into the barbed wire and explode even more paths through it. Snipers had infiltrated into the camp with the first sappers and set up in preselected positions so they could pick off important personnel who survived the initial attack.

Nua, the cute little daughter of Nhual, rolled over in her sleep and clutched the little brown teddy bear that had been given to her by her daddy's friend, me. Her brother shifted on the bamboo-matted bed and stuck his thumb into his mouth. Nhual sat up in a sweat, eyes wide open: Something was wrong, dead wrong. He could sense it. Nhual swung his legs over the edge of his bed, gave his wife a reassuring touch when she stirred, and started to pull on his boots.

The timers went off, and it was as if someone opened a giant door in the ground and unleashed hell for a while. Most of the satchel charges exploded simultaneously, and others, seconds later. Weapons fired all over the camp and more satchel charges were thrown into other bunkers or bunkers where the timers didn't work. NVA sappers scrambled all over the eleven hills of Dak Pek just like an army of invading ants in a village of anthills. As Montagnards ran out of bunkers, they were mowed down, in most cases, from several directions at once. It was not a battle, it was slaughter.

Most of the American team members were killed in their sleep by either the exploding satchel charges or having the bunker cave in on top of them. The human sounds of pain, adrenaline, and panic came from out of the darkness and dust clouds all over the camp. Nhual, his wife, son, and daughter were killed instantly. So were Suet, his wife and two daughters, Tieh, and Mr. Oh and his entire family.

The Dak Pek paymaster, who had shared the bunker with Bon and his wife, along with the LLDB radio operator, waited outside the American team house with M-16s, hoping to pick off any surviving Americans.

Tuan, the lone surviving interpreter, crawled through the small hole in the ground where his bunker had been. He looked all around at the carnage and heard the moans and screams of dying people everywhere. He spotted the two Vietnamese traitors and felt a deep hatred welling up in his chest. An NVA soldier ran beside him in the darkness, and Tuan stuck out his arm and tripped the sapper. He was on him in a millisecond, his Montagnard knife flashing in the moonlight. It passed through the soldier's Adam's apple. Tuan took the man's AK, checked the chamber, and flipped it on automatic.

He stood up and walked slowly forward, barefooted and bare-chested, not caring whether he was going to live or die. The two camp spies stood up staring at him approaching until they could see the evil grin of hatred on his face. Tuan squeezed the trigger of the AK-47 and sent them to hell in a hurry.

One of Commo Willy's seventy-two-foot radio towers lay across the team commander's collapsed bunker and the other lay across the caved-in roof of the American team house. The tunnel system that honeycombed the American hill was totally collapsed, along with almost every team member's bunker, making the surface of the American hill look like the epicenter of an enormous earthquake. The TOC and commo bunker were partially collapsed and on fire. Dust and smoke hung over the entire camp and already thousands of bodies lay everywhere.

Commo Willy heard footsteps running around above his partially collapsed bunker and concluded that death was awaiting him above the ground.

Sergeant Weeks slipped on his ammo belt and tried to figure out how to crawl out of his bunker. Dust grabbed at his lungs and tried to rip each breath to shreds. He moved around the black space, trying to locate a spot where there was a little fresh air. Weeks had to get out—he was the team sergeant. He was the top NCO for the team at Dak Pek.

As Louis L'Amour, the late great western author, used to say, Master Sergeant Thomas Weeks had been "over the mountains and down the river." He was a professional SF NCO and knew what had happened in the opening minutes of the attack. His mind was already calculating what would have to be done without even seeing how much damage there was. He knew by the telltale tinny sounds of AK-47s firing and the sounds of various explosions what were satchel charges, incoming or outgoing weapons firing, and who was winning.

Sergeant Weeks had been both a light- and a heavy-weapons specialist. He could, blindfolded, assemble or disassemble any major firearm in the world. He could fire 60 mm and 81 mm mortars and even a four-deuce without a sight and do it more quickly and more accurately than most mortar specialists using a sight.

He was no longer the weapons man: He was the team operations sergeant. The CO commanded the team, but the team sergeant made it happen. There was no CO now or XO and Sergeant Weeks had to find out who there was, what he had to work with, whom he was facing, and how he could manage to kick their ass. He felt some sandbags and started yanking on them. He would get out or die trying, and if he had to do that, he decided, some Communists were going under with him. He angrily jerked and clawed at sandbags and chunks of concrete.

Commo Willy heard tons of footsteps and AKs being fired above his partially collapsed bunker, but he had the same thoughts as Sergeant Weeks. Suddenly, he remembered a case of hand grenades he had prepared for an emergency and placed next to his now-destroyed single-side band radio. He also had to find a radio that worked. Thick black smoke billowed out of the TOC and commo room, but by crawling on his belly he finally made it down the underground tunnel to the commo room and felt around until his hands located the case of grenades. He grabbed them as if they were a life jacket and he was a drowning man. Commo Willy crawled back down the hallway toward his bunker. Just beyond that, he saw the collapsed emergency medical bunker and knew the team medic, Sergeant Jim Erickson, was inside there, probably crushed.

He heard some NVA laughing and firing at the top of his bunker steps, and he started shoving hand grenades into his fatigue trouser pockets. He got hold of his M-16 and harness, along with his .38 special, which he tucked into the back of his pants. He looked up the half-destroyed stairs leading up into the night air, where he still heard the laughing NVA soldiers.

Commo Willy thought about his mom back in Florida and the supposed curse on his family. He pulled the pin on an HE grenade and held it in his hand.

"Fuck it," he muttered and threw the grenade up into the night air.

Ducking back behind the wall, he jacked a round into the chamber of his M-16, waited for the grenade to explode, then charged up the stairs into the midst of his enemies. He opened up with the M-16 on automatic and sprayed around in every direction, NVA soldiers falling under the firepower. He ran back into the bunker, grabbed the case of grenades, and dragged it up the steps. Dropping the M-16, he started throwing hand grenades at NVA who swarmed everywhere.

When Commo Willy took off out of the bunker, a sapper decided to throw another satchel charge into the TOC to finish its demolition. He pulled the pin on the detonator fuse and tossed the bag of explosives into the bunker and froze at the sound of a voice.

"Turn around, Commie asshole," came the calm voice of Sergeant Weeks.

The sapper turned and his eyes opened wide as saucers as the NCO's weapon blasted into his chest. The NVA flew backward down the steps and landed on the satchel charge. It exploded, and so did the sapper.

Sergeant Weeks saw Commo Willy throwing grenades and they waved at each other.

Weeks yelled, "Find a radio . . . dust-offs, reinforcements, whatever you can think of!"

Commo Willy gave a wave, a nod, and threw a grenade toward some NVA in the drive below the latrine. His arm caught, however, on something sticking out of the sandbags and the grenade fell in front of him. He quickly deserted the partially destroyed mortar bunker and the case of grenades by diving in the opposite direction. The hand grenade exploded, but fortunately outside the sandbagged bunker.

Williams grabbed his weapon and a couple more grenades and set about to search for a radio. He was teased by every man on the team about not sleeping. Commo

Willy was always on the radio, and when he wasn't there, he was making a new backup system of some sort. He used commo wire to run through the American hill's tunnels to make emergency backup radio antennas. He had also dug, by hand, an emergency bunker, under the TOC, containing a five-KW generator. Commo Willy was smart enough to dig that bunker and put the generator in without letting anyone but Americans know about his project. Along with the generator, he hid an underground AN/PRC-74 radio and an AN/GRC-109 radio near the TOC. He found both of these and the generator working.

Commo Willy started transmitting on CW and got Kontum on the air. He then switched to voice and let them know that the camp had been overrun, and he requested any help they could get, especially medevacs. He was ordered to destroy all radios and sensitive items, and get the hell out of there.

The Fifth Special Forces Group had a unit of some of the toughest fighters in Vietnam, mainly Yards, who were Airborne-qualified and whose goal was to go into "hot" A-, B-, or C-teams to rescue people and provide reinforcements. Then each of the C-teams in the four Corps areas similarly had a tough unit like this, and each B-team also had such a unit. These units were called Mobile Strike Forces, but were referred to, by everyone, as Mike Forces. Minutes after the call came in from Don Williams, the Kontum and Pleiku Mike Forces started preparations to go in and save the Americans and try to repel the attack.

Lee, the barmaid in the team house, had taken over as camp cook and had married the intel sergeant. They made it out of their bunker but were separated from Weeks and Williams.

The light-weapons man also got separated from them and was gravely wounded.

Williams started destroying radios and electronic equipment with thermite grenades while Sergeant Weeks gathered up the few remaining Yards and set up a perimeter around the half-collapsed team house. The entire scene was brightly lighted by flames shooting up from the LLDB's bamboo team house. *Dai-uy* Hoe had been gravely wounded in the first attack and his wife and one of his two children were killed. Most of the members of the tough recon platoon were blown up in their sleep.

Weeks crawled, ran, and fought his way all over the American hill checking the bunkers of every man, sadly finding most of them dead. He and Commo Willy met at the southeast corner of the American hill, facing the LLVC hill, and found themselves staring at the barrel of their own 106 millimeter recoilless rifle, being manned by a squad of NVA. The NVA had loaded it with *fléchette* rounds, which were thousands of steel darts fired like a giant shotgun. They fired at the two Americans from one hundred yards away. Weeks just stared at them, hands on his hips, and laughed. They fired again.

The team sergeant turned to Williams and said, "The dumb bastards are trying to shoot us with *fléchette* rounds. No fucking way can they touch us!"

As one, the two NCOs grinned at each other and opened fire, hosing down the NVA with their rifles. They both took off looking for more Americans.

The two Americans and a handful of wounded Montagnards ran from position to position all night long, repelling the attack of thousands of NVA. Sometimes they made light probes, and several times they came in waves, but the two Americans and their friends apparently had God in their foxholes with them.

Dawn came and the total destruction became very obvious. With dawn came dust-offs and the Kontum and Pleiku Mike Forces, as well as a Fourth Division Infantry Battalion out of Dak To. They were all combat-assaulted into the foothills ringing Dak Pek, while the medevacs came into the camp and picked up some of the wounded.

Commo Willy and Sergeant Weeks kept checking

their expedient perimeter and heard a groan. They grabbed a flashlight and ran down into the hallway going to Commo Willy's bunker. The groan came from beyond that. They found a hole in the ruins of the collapsed medical bunker, and they saw a face looking back at them. Dirt all over his face, and glasses cracked and twisted on an angle, team medic Jim Erickson smiled at them. They dug him out.

The trio made it to the team house and sat there awhile, when suddenly Sergeant Weeks jumped up, staring out the door.

He grabbed his rifle, yanked the door off the hinges in anger, and growled, "What the fuck!"

Williams and Erickson followed him outside and saw three NVA standing at the camp flagpole. They had removed the American and Vietnamese flags and had a North Vietnamese flag halfway up the pole.

Weeks lost it.

He stomped forward and yelled, "Nobody touches the American flag, you Communist motherfuckers!"

His angry words snapped their heads toward the furious master sergeant, standing in the middle of the driveway, totally exposed, shoulders back. The three NVA soldiers grabbed for their AK-47s, but Weeks had other plans.

He yelled, "Fuck you!" and opened fire on automatic.

The three sappers didn't even get a chance to fire a return shot but sprawled in the dust of the camp parade ground, lying in their own blood.

Without looking at the two openmouthed NCOs, he snapped over his shoulder, "Fuck this shit! Come on!"

With Weeks leading the way, the two NCOs followed, along with the Montagnards. Weeks stomped to the camp flagpole and, with the others forming a perimeter around the pole, he pulled down the NVA flag and set it on fire with a Zippo lighter. He picked up the American flag off the ground and hoisted it up the flagpole, not paying any attention to the snipers' bullets whizzing around his ears.

Completing that, he said, "Okay, it's over. We got to kill all these bastards. It's too late for Dak Pek."

The ever-sentimental but tough Tuan had a tear in his eye. They followed Sergeant Weeks as he led and fought his way across several occupied hills to the south end of the camp. They fought their way to the top of the hill for Charlie Company, the most southern position in Dak Pek.

Weeks had had it and knew the camp was not only destroyed but lost as well. NVA swarmed all over the American and Vietnamese hills. The camp was a lost cause, so the men concentrated their fire on any NVA that tried to make it to the flagpole to remove the red-white-and-blue flag waving so proudly in the blowing, acrid smoke. A FAC flew overhead and Weeks grabbed the mike to the radio Commo Willy brought. He called for extraction helicopters and gave his location.

Then he called the FAC, "Bird Dog, this is the Dak Pek element on the ground, over."

"Yeah, man, I got an eyeball on you, you the only ones left, over."

There was a long pregnant pause and then Weeks said, "Roger, over."

"Damn. Well, guys, I got all kinds of birds on station. I'll try to keep their heads down for you guys till they pull you out, over."

"Not what I want," Weeks said. "Can you put an Arc Light in on us without hitting us? Over."

"This is Bird Dog Two-four. Maybe and maybe not. They aren't too accurate, you know. Over."

Weeks didn't hesitate. "Doesn't matter, it's got to be done. Bring it in ASAP, over."

Sergeant Weeks had just asked the US Air Force to bring in a B-52 carpet bombing strike to level Dak Pek.

The FAC responded, "I already have the big birds on station, because of the call-in on this last night, but are you sure of this, over?"

"Do it. Out," Weeks replied firmly and without hesitation.

The voice that came back was sad, "Wilco, good luck and God bless you, son. Out."

Ten minutes later, the NCOs watched and held their ears while a B-52 strike, an "Arc Light," poured 500-pound bombs on the northern half of the camp, as if some giant in the sky were sprinkling grass seed on the sod. The 500-pound bombs rained in, destroying everything, bouncing the Americans up and down, and demolishing numerous NVA in the process. Apparently the NVA didn't figure that anyone would have the guts to call in a B-52 strike on their own position, but the NVA forgot they had fucked with the US Army Special Forces. Now they would have to dance to the piper, the tune of a B-52 Overture.

Choppers landed and extracted Weeks, Erickson, and Williams. Williams's chopper just started to lift off when his pet dog, which he inherited from me, jumped onto the chopper. The weapons man, intel sergeant, and Lee had got out earlier.

The Mike Force and the Fourth Division units walked into the ruins of Dak Pek and the stench of the thousands of decaying bodies couldn't be filtered out with a scarf, kerchief, or anything. Miles away in Kontum Commo Willy gave a Montagnard named Jolly a gift, a little black-and-white dog from Dak Pek.

The dog named Ambush was a gift for Plar, the little Montagnard girl I had wanted to adopt. The little girl who had been viciously taken away by hate and discrimination. Plar was a sweet little girl who hadn't grown enough to learn to fear or hate. She spoke Jeh, but liked dolls, candy, and playing grownup, simply another innocent victim of a war of ignorance, as are all wars. A war that is still going on.

And so ended the safest A-camp in Vietnam, where nobody really was safe. Where the front line was how far you could throw a grenade or send your bullets. Where the front line was where trust and loyalty were bordered by treason and espionage. Where men and women did what they believed was right, while their friends and neighbors screamed at them for following their own beliefs. Where the slaves were our true allies, and the masters were our Benedict Arnolds. Where SF stood tall, warriors against the masses, unfailing in their courage or convictions. Where the NVA finally had to dance to a deadly tune: the strains of the B-52 Overture.

Supplement

COMMO WILLY BROKE the supposed curse on his family and had a long and distinguished career in the US Army Special Forces. Highly decorated from the Vietnam War, he served in Okinawa, Thailand, Taiwan, England, Germany, and the United States, including work as an instructor on both the HALO and the SCUBA committees. A master sergeant, on the list for sergeant major, he was accidentally shot in the spine and paralyzed in Lebanon on January 9, 1985, exactly five days after completing twenty years in the service. Medically retired and bound to a wheelchair, Don Williams now lives a happy life with his wife and daughters in western Kansas.

Joe Dietrich, also a highly decorated Vietnam veteran, currently serves as a full bird colonel with the US Army Special Forces at MacDill Air Force Base, Florida. Like me, he has two sons who are champion black belts in Tae Kwon Do.

Another highly decorated veteran, Tom Weeks, retired from Special Forces a sergeant major and was living happily with his family in Texas, at last word.

Larry Crotsley left the Army after Vietnam and is a happily married father of two girls and president of a trucking company in New Jersey.

Jim Erickson had a distinguished military career and was last seen as a first sergeant in Fort Devens, Massachusetts.

Larry Vosen is leading a happy family life and is a regional manager of auto parts stores in southern California. He lives in Riverside.

It was rumored that Charlie Telfair retired an E-8 or E-9 and is a college professor in the South.

Tuan and the surviving Montagnards are still in hiding in the jungles of Vietnam, Cambodia, and Laos. Some have been caught and executed by the Vietnamese, while others have been put into slave labor gangs for the government. Some have joined FULRO fighting forces hiding in the jungle and striking out on behalf of the Montagnard's cause. This is being done on their own without the support of any government. The Montagnard is disappearing at the rate of an average of 275 people per day.

The whereabouts and disposition of others mentioned in this book are not known.

Montagnard Foundation, Inc.

EADERS WHO WOULD LIKE to make a charitable
contribution to the Montagnards may do so by
sending their tax-free donations to the Montagnard
Foundation, Inc., a South Carolina nonprofit corporation.

Make checks payable and send them to:

Montagnard Foundation, Inc.

PO Box 17064

Spartanburg, South Carolina 29301

All the monies collected are handled solely by
Montagnards and are used totally for the benefit, educa-
tion, and assistance of Montagnards both here and
abroad.

About the Author

DON BENDELL IS A former captain in the US Army Special Forces. A graduate of Infantry OCS and also the US Army Intelligence School at Fort Holabird, Maryland, he was a member of the Third, Fifth, Sixth, and Seventh Special Forces Groups. This included a 1968–1969 tour as an A-Team XO–CA/PO at Dak Pek in the northwestern corner of II Corps in South Vietnam's Central Highlands region. He is senior advisor to the president of the FULRO, the Montagnards' resistance movement; after leaving the Army he returned to Fort Bragg in 1974 and 1975 as a civilian karate instructor.

Don lives in the mountains of southern Colorado with his black belt wife, Shirley, and two of his six children.

He still works tirelessly as senior advisor to the president of the Montagnards, trying to provide refugee relief and assistance to them.